180
Devotions
FOR
WHEN LIFE
IS HARD

180 Devotions
FOR
WHEN LIFE IS HARD

Wisdom &
Encouragement
for Guys

BARBOUR
PUBLISHING

Contributors to *180 Devotions for When Life Is Hard:*

Bob Evenhouse
Elijah Adkins
Lee Warren
Paul Kent
Zech Haynes

© 2023 by Barbour Publishing, Inc.

Print ISBN 978-1-63609-574-5

Published by Barbour Publishing, Inc., 1810 Barbour Drive, Uhrichsville, Ohio 44683, www.barbourbooks.com

Our mission is to inspire the world with the life-changing message of the Bible.

Member of the
Evangelical Christian
Publishers Association

Printed in the United States of America.

Introduction

It's a tough world. . . but God is far stronger.

When you need a boost, read *180 Devotions for When Life Is Hard.* Here is wisdom and encouragement for teen guys in scores of powerful entries.

As a Christian teen, you have the advantage of knowing God personally—but life still throws some real challenges your way. These devotions cover topics including

- family
- fitting in
- health
- persistence
- self-esteem
- the future
- and much more

Whatever life brings your way, *180 Devotions for When Life Is Hard* offers truthful, practical words to encourage and inspire your soul. It's a tough world, but God is far stronger. Read on to know Him better!

There's Always Hope

I recall this to my mind; therefore I have hope. It is because of the LORD's mercies that we are not consumed, because His compassions do not fail.
LAMENTATIONS 3:21–22 SKJV

• •

Talk about tough times! Jeremiah knew how hard life could be.

As a teenager, he became God's prophet to Judah. The people were sinful, and Jeremiah got the job of saying that. They weren't happy.

Jeremiah was insulted, beaten, imprisoned . . .and ultimately ignored. God finally sent King Nebuchadnezzar's Babylonian army to overrun Judah. Having sown disrespect toward God, the people reaped a bitter harvest of captivity and death.

Jeremiah experienced it all—and all alone. God had warned him things would get so bad that he shouldn't marry or have kids (Jeremiah 16:1–4).

But even in such times, Jeremiah could write the words above. God is always compassionate. His kindness is "new every morning" (Lamentation 3:23 SKJV), His faithfulness "great" to those who humbly follow Him.

No matter how crazy life gets, stick with God. He'll carry you through the worst of times. Things *will* get better—whether in this life or in heaven to come.

• •

Lord, give me Jeremiah's perspective when things get crazy. I need Your hope!

Cosmic Struggles

[God] has delivered us from the power of darkness and has translated us to the kingdom of His dear Son.
COLOSSIANS 1:13 SKJV

. . . .

Most of us have grown up with fictional portrayals of good versus evil. The light and dark sides of the Force in *Star Wars*, Gandalf and Sauron in *The Lord of the Rings*, superheroes and supervillains in the Marvel films—the big-screen conflict thrills our souls.

What many of us don't realize, however, is that such a struggle is actually happening—and our hearts are the battleground.

Reality itself is ruled by God. But lurking in the shadows is Satan's horde of demonic forces, silently twisting the hearts of anyone who lets them. As Christians, we are on the side of good—and we must stay alert, armored spiritually, ready for the relentless attacks of the enemy.

If we have followed Jesus by faith, we are already part of God's kingdom. And once the thin veil between this life and the next is pulled away, we'll see with our eyes what we now recognize only by faith.

. . . .

Lord, may I always be ready to battle for Your kingdom. Protect me in the fight and prepare me for eternity, when the power of darkness is ended forever.

A Safe Place

There is strong trust in the fear of the Lord,
and His children will have a safe place.
PROVERBS 14:26 NLV

Our world is not a safe place. Mass shootings occur regularly. Human trafficking ruins lives. *Pandemic* has become a common term. Your generation has experienced more danger than many before. But you don't need to live in fear of what might happen in this life. You have the hope of eternity.

Jesus once said, "Do not be afraid of them who kill the body. They are not able to kill the soul. But fear Him Who is able to destroy both soul and body in hell" (Matthew 10:28 NLV).

As you fear God—that is, as you respect Him for His holiness and power—He provides a safe place for you. He's got your back: "The name of the Lord is a strong tower. The man who does what is right runs into it and is safe" (Proverbs 18:10 NLV).

By trusting in Jesus, your place in heaven is secure— more secure than anything this life has to offer. You can live confidently, knowing that God is your safe place.

Lord, I fear and trust You. I know that
in Your name, I find safety.

Life's Dilemmas

*"Who knows whether you have come to
the kingdom for such a time as this?"*
ESTHER 4:14 SKJV

• •

As the Jews' fate hung in the balance, Queen Esther found herself in a terrifying dilemma: say nothing and watch her people die, or approach the king for help and risk her own death. She called on the one person she could absolutely trust for advice—Mordecai, her cousin-turned-adoptive-parent.

Mordecai first acknowledged God's providence. "If you altogether remain quiet at this time, then relief and deliverance shall arise for the Jews from another place." Then he warned Esther that her inaction could have devastating results: "But you and your father's house shall be destroyed." Finally, he ended with a subtle call to action: "And who knows whether you have come to the kingdom for such a time as this?" (All quotes in this paragraph from Esther 4:14 SKJV).

Sometimes, the reassurance of a trusted friend is all a person needs to stand up for God and His truth. Do you have that kind of friend? Are you that kind of friend? Ask God to guide you in Esther's way *before* any crisis strikes.

• •

*Lord, give me and my Christian friends the wisdom
and strength to honor You in life's dilemmas.*

A Great Full Life

• •

Our culture has plenty to say about living your best life: "Follow your dreams!" "You only live once!" "You do you!" Do you notice the common element in each statement? They're all centered on selfishness.

Jesus once said of Himself, "The Son of Man came not to be cared for. He came to care for others. He came to give His life" (Matthew 20:28 NLV). Jesus had all the power in the universe, but He came to serve and to give.

This concept of selfless living might sound boring in comparison to pursuing fame, fortune, freedom, and fun. But Jesus said following Him would be far better than emphasizing your own dreams: "I came so they might have life, a great full life" (John 10:10 NLV).

That's a promise. Why not test it out?

• •

Lord, help me to put off my own desires in favor or Yours. I know that Your ways are the best ways!

Refreshed and Renewed

As the deer desires rivers of water,
so my soul desires You, O God.
PSALM 42:1 NLV

· ·

At times in life, you'll feel tired, weak, dried out. That's just a given in a broken world filled with trouble and pain.

The answer, not surprisingly, is God. Whoever wrote Psalm 42 recognized that the Lord would be like the river that refreshed the tongue of a desperate, panting deer. God is like the oasis that restores life to a dying man in the sun-baked desert.

Even in the best of times, this world cannot completely satisfy. Only the God who created you, knows you, loves you, and redeems you through the life and work of His Son, Jesus, can fulfill your deepest longings.

That may be hard to believe when every influence of the world screams otherwise. But deep down, you know you were made for God. Why not spend some extra time in His Word today. See if He doesn't slake the thirst in your soul.

· ·

Lord God, I need to be refreshed and renewed.
Please pour Your living water into my spirit.

Jesus Understands

Because Jesus was tempted as we are and
suffered as we do, He understands us and He
is able to help us when we are tempted.
HEBREWS 2:18 NLV

• •

Jesus had to be like humanity in every way so He could be our merciful and faithful High Priest (Hebrews 2:17). He's a Savior who can relate to the suffering and heartache of His people. He knows hunger, weariness, persecution, mockery, and temptation, all from personal experience. So He knows exactly how *you* feel in your current challenge.

Think about that for a minute. The God of the universe stepped into a human body and suffered—not only to save your soul in eternity but also to help you right here, right now. He knows exactly what you're facing, even if nobody else does. He's just waiting for you to call His name for help. Don't be afraid—He understands!

• •

Lord Jesus, I'm thankful that You understand every
temptation and challenge I face. Draw me close to
Yourself and give me the strength to rise above.

The Bigger Picture

*"You thought evil against me, but
God meant it for good."*
GENESIS 50:20 SKJV

• •

If anyone knows how hard life can get, it's Joseph.

He was just seventeen when his jealous brothers sold him into slavery. Then in Egypt, his master's wife falsely accused him of harassment—and poor Joseph was thrown into prison for two years.

Do you sometimes feel like Joseph? No, not sold into slavery by your siblings (hopefully not, anyway!), but experiencing plenty of tough trials otherwise. Considering the typical day-to-day inconveniences, classroom drama, family challenges, and the looming phantom of adulthood, life can feel like a boiling sea of chaos and stress—just as it did for Joseph.

But thankfully, Joseph's story didn't end there. Through a divinely orchestrated sequence of events, this poor, outcast teenager ended up as Pharaoh's right-hand man! Joseph was able to provide food for countless people—including his own brothers—when a catastrophic famine struck the region.

When you find yourself on the receiving end of life's punches, remember this: your story isn't finished yet.

• •

*Lord, I know You're working things out for my good,
even when it feels like everything is wrong. Thank
You for making me part of Your master plan.*

It's Crazy Out There

"O LORD, how long shall I cry, and You will not hear, even cry out to You, 'Violence!' and You will not save? Why do You show me iniquity and cause me to behold grievance?"

HABAKKUK 1:2–3 SKJV

• •

Sometimes life is hard due to tough personal circumstances. You or a loved one is sick. Your family is having financial problems. You really, really like this girl who doesn't seem to know you exist. . . .

At other times, life is hard because the whole world is broken. Wars and natural disasters destroy lives. Abuse and oppression run rampant. The things people say and do just don't even make sense.

That's how Habakkuk felt, centuries before Jesus was born. He begged God to fix the craziness of his world, but his prayers seemed to bounce off the ceiling.

Good news: God does hear our prayers. And, in the background, He's directing all things to His own glory. He has a vision for a perfect resolution, and "though it delays, wait for it, because it will surely come" (Habakkuk 2:3 SKJV).

• •

Heavenly Father, help me to trust in Your perfect plan. I know You will do right!

You Are Free!

*What does this mean? Are we to keep on
sinning so that God will give us more of His
loving-favor? No, not at all! We are dead to
sin. How then can we keep on living in sin?*
ROMANS 6:1–2 NLV

"I am *free!*" Go ahead, say that out loud. There's nothing wrong with speaking truth to yourself. If you know Jesus as Savior, you are free. You don't have to beat yourself up when you sin or stress over anyone else's expectations of you. When life gets tough—and it does—it's great to know that you are free in Christ.

When God looks at you, He doesn't see sin—He sees the righteousness of Jesus in you. He sees your freedom, your redemption by Jesus' blood. So start looking at yourself the way your heavenly Father does. Yes, you'll still make mistakes, but He's ready and willing to forgive them for Jesus' sake. And He has the strength to break the power of sin in your life forever.

*Lord Jesus, help me to see myself the way Your
Father sees me. I am free from sin and shame!*

When Life Feels Heavy

*"If only my trials and troubles were weighed! They
would weigh more than the sand of the seas."*
Job 6:2–3 NLV

• •

Job was a man who lived right before God but faced
terrible struggles. Ever felt that way? Sometimes you're
following God faithfully, but bad things keep happening. You might even ask Job's famous question: *Why?*

As followers of Jesus, we are enemies of the world.
He told us as much—but He also offered encouragement. "I have told you these things so you may have
peace in Me," He said. "In the world you will have much
trouble. But take hope! I have power over the world!"
(John 16:33 NLV).

Notice that Jesus didn't say you *might* face troubles, but rather that you *will*. And He didn't say He
wished He had power over the world, but that He does.
When life feels heavy, remind yourself that Jesus has
things well under control.

• •

*God, I thank you that in Jesus I can overcome
my most difficult life experiences.*

Preparing for Adulthood

"Is not the LORD your God with you? . . . Now set your heart and your soul to seek the LORD your God."
1 CHRONICLES 22:18–19 SKJV

• •

The teen years are great—or at least they should be. You're old enough to go places and do things you couldn't do as a little kid. There's a whole world of opportunity opening up before you. It won't be long before you're a full-fledged adult, making your own way in life.

Okay, so some of that actually sounds a bit scary. And that's why the teen years, for all of their benefits, can be stressful. There are so many decisions to make. What if you choose poorly? Will you wreck your whole life by picking the wrong elective in tenth grade?

Today's scripture contains the words of King David, preparing his son Solomon to follow him on the throne. As a father, David was rightly teaching his son. But the teaching pointed Solomon to the source of all wisdom and help, God Himself. Yes, God was certainly with Solomon, as He is with you. "Now set your heart and your soul to seek the LORD your God."

• •

Heavenly Father, I need You to guide me into adulthood. And please help me to enjoy the process!

Walk Rightly

He who is right in his walk is sure in his steps, but he who takes the wrong way will be found out.
PROVERBS 10:9 NLV

. . . .

The world will tell you to "be true to yourself"—to be proud of whatever you desire, even if it goes against the Word of God. Actually, the world will be *especially* eager for you to do that.

Supposedly, you'll develop a healthy self-esteem by "living your truth." But the Bible has a very different view. Scripture says if you want to be your best self, you need to walk rightly—obediently—before God.

Truth is only found in Jesus Christ (John 14:6), and He makes you a new creature (2 Corinthians 5:17). That's something to be proud of! Christians fight against their sinful desires, knowing that as they do, they'll discover who God really intended them to be.

Is that easy? No. But when you "fight the good fight of faith," you'll also "take hold of the life that lasts forever" (1 Timothy 6:12 NLV).

. . . .

Lord, I want to be sure of who I am.
Please help me to walk rightly with You.

Our Excuses, His Strength

*But Moses said to the Lord, "See, the people of Israel
have not listened to me. How then will Pharaoh
listen to me? I am not able to speak well."*
EXODUS 6:12 NLV

• •

How would you react if someone you respected asked
you to do something beyond your ability? Would you
try anyway? Many people would probably just say no.

Now imagine the person making the request
was God.

The Lord wanted Moses to confront Pharaoh, the
ruler of Egypt, and tell him to free the Israelites from
their slavery. Though God showed Moses miraculous
signs (the burning bush, a staff turned into a snake),
Moses still had trouble accepting God's plan. Moses
was focused on what *he* could do. God wanted to use
a human's weakness to prove His own divine power.

The next time you have an opportunity to be bold
for God, step forward. Remember, it's not you doing
the work but God Himself accomplishing His plans
through you.

• •

*Father, mold me into a person who says yes to You,
no matter how challenging the situation might seem.*

Be Ready

Finally, my brothers, be strong in the Lord and in the power of His might. Put on the whole armor of God, that you may be able to stand against the schemes of the devil. For we wrestle not against flesh and blood but against principalities, against powers, against the rulers of the darkness of this world, against spiritual wickedness in high places.
EPHESIANS 6:10–12 SKJV

If your life isn't hard right now, be ready. . .tough things will come. You remember that Jesus promised trouble, right? "In the world you shall have tribulation" (John 16:33 SKJV).

Trials should be no surprise to us. So make the effort now to be prepared for them.

The apostle Paul told believers to put on the whole armor of God (Ephesians 6:13–17). You wear a belt of truth, the knowledge you get from scripture. There's the breastplate of righteousness, your standing with God through Jesus. You carry a shield of faith, that knocks down the "fiery darts" of Satan. "Putting on" is a conscious thing—you have to intentionally choose to study God's Word and think—carefully and consistently—about what it says.

When you do, you'll be ready for whatever troubles this world throws at you.

Lord, please help me to don Your armor!

God Weeps with Us

Jesus wept.
JOHN 11:35 SKJV

• •

We may think it was Lazarus' death that moved Jesus to tears. But John 11:33 (SKJV) reveals the true cause: "When Jesus saw [Mary] weeping, and the Jews who came with her also weeping, He groaned in the spirit and was troubled." God in the flesh wasn't grieving for Himself—He was moved by the pain He saw in others.

Guys don't always like to admit they're hurting. Crying seems like a sign of weakness. But in our darkest moments, when life seems so unfair and brutal and cruel that we can barely think, know that God Himself is weeping for you. He knows and feels your pain. And though He also knows it won't last forever, He will never look down on your suffering.

When the most loving, compassionate Being in the universe saw His friends in emotional pain, tears flowed freely. He knew full well that in a few short minutes, Lazarus would live again—but for the moment, this grief would not go unnoticed.

God recognizes your pain too.

• •

Father, thank You for sharing my pain. Help me
to feel Your presence during my darkest hour.

Live Differently

*For everything that is in the world does not
come from the Father. The desires of our flesh
and the things our eyes see and want and the
pride of this life come from the world.*
1 John 2:16 NLV

• •

You don't have to be out on your own to feel the world
pulling you away from God. From a young age, you've
seen advertisements that try to convince you some
thing—a toy, a video game, a kind of clothing, whatever—
will make you happy. As you get older, you'll hear that
you need money, fame, or sex to be complete. But
these messages are not from the Father.

How does the Bible tell you to live? "Keep your
lives free from the love of money. Be happy with what
you have. God has said, 'I will never leave you or let
you be alone' " (Hebrews 13:5 NLV). "Christian brothers,
I ask you from my heart to give your bodies to God
because of His loving-kindness to us. Let your bodies
be a living and holy gift given to God. He is pleased
with this kind of gift. This is the true worship that you
should give Him" (Romans 12:1 NLV).

In other words, live differently than the world
around you.

• •

*Lord, may I be satisfied with what You give
me, willing to sacrifice all for You.*

God Thinks You're Cool

*The L*ORD *your God in the midst of you is mighty. He will save; He will rejoice over you with joy. He will rest in His love; He will rejoice over you with singing.*
ZEPHANIAH 3:17 SKJV

So maybe you're not the most popular guy at school. Maybe you're not the best looking. Maybe you lack athletic or artistic or musical ability. Maybe you tripped in front of the cool kids' table at lunchtime. None of that matters to God.

If you have accepted His Son, Jesus, as your Lord and Savior, God thinks you're cool. And not only cool, but worthy of His attention and love *forever*. God didn't choose you for any particular desirability of your own. But when you humbly followed Jesus, the Father began to see you *through* His Son. And Jesus' perfection overwhelms any flaws in your life.

You don't need to be a star in this world. When God thinks you're cool, *you're cool*. Knowing that, why not reach out to help others know Him too? They'd enjoy God's rejoicing over them as well.

Heavenly Father, help me to accept my high position as a follower of Your Son, Jesus.

Good Wins. . .Ultimately

So God punished Abimelech for the sin
he had done against his father.
JUDGES 9:56 NLV

∙∙∙

Thanos, Hitler, Voldemort, Nero. Whether fictional characters or real-life bad guys, they're known for their evil actions. The biblical Abimelech was one of them.

Out of extreme selfishness, he killed *seventy* of his brothers so he could rule over Israel. Only his youngest brother, Jotham, survived the purge. Can you imagine the questions in Jotham's mind as Abimelech held power? How could God allow evil to win?

We've all seen justice delayed. Maybe you've even asked the question, "Why do good things happen to bad people?" Just remember that the Bible teaches that God is still in control. Without question, justice will win. God eventually punished Abimelech by turning the hearts of his countrymen against him.

God has His own time and techniques, but He will make sure that every wrong is righted. Hang tough. . . He'll make sure good wins, ultimately.

∙∙∙

Father, help me to remember that You are
the perfect judge. You don't allow evil to go
unpunished. Keep me always doing good.

You're Not Alone

God saw the people of Israel and He cared about them.
EXODUS 2:25 NLV

• •

Have you ever felt alone in a crowd? What about in class, on a team, or even in your home? Life can seem very lonely, especially for Christians in a not-so-Christian environment. Sometimes it feels like there is no one to turn to.

The ancient Israelites certainly felt out of step with the surrounding Egyptian culture. They were expected to follow God's rules and stand apart from their neighbors. Over time, they began to suffer severe persecution—to the point of being made into slaves. But "God heard their groaning, and God remembered His covenant with Abraham, with Isaac, and with Jacob" (Exodus 2:24 SKJV).

Long ago, God had compassion on His people and provided deliverance. He still does that. When you feel alone or persecuted, cry out to the Lord. He is sure to hear and respond to you too.

• •

Lord, sometimes I feel alone. Please give me the encouragement and energy to continue following You in a troubled and troubling culture.

The First, Scary Step

*Put to death therefore the parts of
your body that are on the earth.*
Colossians 3:5 skjv

• •

In fictional works, the "hero's journey" serves as a template for the protagonist's progression through the story. Near the beginning of the journey, the hero is faced with a pivotal choice: leave behind everything he knows and loves in an epic quest to discover meaning, or stay behind and remain engulfed in mundane familiarity.

Often, the choice is agonizing. Adventure means stepping outside one's comfort zone—tearing down one's old self and welcoming the new.

As a child of God, you're part in the greatest story ever told—a cosmic, sweeping tale of good versus evil, bravery in the face of persecution, and ultimately, redemption. But to participate in this story, you must first make a choice: are you willing to kill off "the parts of your body that are on the earth"? Are you willing to cut the ropes that tie you down to this old, tired planet in favor of a kingdom that will never die?

Your adventure awaits. . .

• •

*Lord, help me to follow Your storyline. I know the
journey won't be easy, but You'll always be by my side.*

Learned Obedience

*During the time Jesus lived on earth, He prayed
and asked God with loud cries and tears.
Jesus' prayer was to God Who was able to save
Him from death. God heard Christ because
Christ honored God. Even being God's Son, He
learned to obey by the things He suffered.*
HEBREWS 5:7–8 NLV

When you disobey your parents, you probably suffer some sort of punishment. Over time, you learn to obey. So it is with the Christian life. Suffering is meant to teach us obedience.

An old-time Bible commentator put it this way: Jesus "has set us an example, and has shown that the most perfect obedience may be manifested in the deepest sorrows of the body and the soul. Hence, learn that one of the objects of affliction is to lead us 'to obey God.' "

Are you going through some "sorrow" of body or soul? Physical sickness or inability, the loss of a loved one, financial or spiritual or relationship struggles—all these sorrows are meant to show you your limitations and point out your need for Christ.

Jesus Himself learned obedience by things He suffered. You should too.

*Lord, please use my current sorrows
to teach me obedience.*

When Your Heart Aches

The Lord is near to those who have a broken heart.
And He saves those who are broken in spirit.
PSALM 34:18 NLV

No one is immune to heartache. When you live in a broken, sinful world, tough things are bound to happen. Grandparents decline and pass away. Parents get cancer, lose jobs, or divorce. Girlfriends break up and walk away. You're cut from the basketball team. That prestigious college rejects your application.

There's no way to avoid the mental and emotional hardships of this life. But when they slam you like a Category 5 hurricane, you have a shelter to run to.

God cares deeply for the brokenhearted. When your spirit is snapped in two, He steps in to save. He's eager to share His consolation because He knows pain.

As God in the flesh, Jesus suffered throughout His life on earth—but especially in the crucifixion. And God the Father felt the searing pain of turning away from Jesus as He bore the sins of the entire world.

When your heart aches, know that you have a God who understands. And He promises, one day, that every tear will be wiped away.

Father, when my heart is broken and my spirit crushed, let me feel Your presence and peace.

The In-Between

As they were gathered together with Him, He told them, "Do not leave Jerusalem. Wait for what the Father has promised. You heard Me speak of this."
ACTS 1:4 NLV

• •

Sometimes we just have to wait. Maybe you're stuck in traffic. Maybe your parents have set an age for getting your own phone or dating. Maybe you're anticipating a response from a college application. Waiting can make us feel restless and anxious. It's tough.

And yet the idea of waiting appears all through the Bible. The word *wait* appears over two hundred times in the New Life Version, sometimes with a promise, like this one from Lamentations 3:25: "The Lord is good to those who wait for Him, to the one who looks for Him."

One of Jesus' last instructions to His loyal disciples was to wait—in the city that had so recently demanded and witnessed His death. But there was a promise in that command as well; as they obeyed, God would provide them with the Holy Spirit.

Whatever you're waiting for, keep trusting and obeying God in the in-between. He will make sure your wait is worth it.

• •

Lord, in this period of waiting, be nearby.
Provide comfort, encouragement, and patience.

Face-to-Face

Having many things to write to you, I would not write with paper and ink, but I trust to come to you and speak face to face, that our joy may be full.
2 JOHN 12 SKJV

• •

A long, face-to-face conversation. When's the last time you had one? Today? Yesterday? Last week?

According to a recent survey, nearly half of American teens are online "almost constantly." Combine this with countless other studies that uncover correlations between social media use and poor mental health, and. . .well, you can see where this is going.

The truth is, people need other people. Images and words on a flat surface just don't cut it. The apostle John recognized this nearly two thousand years ago. He certainly loved writing to fellow Christians, but he wanted above all else to *see* them. That was the only way to make their joy full.

Today's world is crazy enough already—why make it worse? When life is hard, you need human interaction just as much as your body needs food and water.

Don't settle for "likes" and "follows" when you can share the love of God with others.

• •

Lord, help me live the way You intended me to—by walking with others and shining Your light for all to see.

When You Lack

[Mary's] first son was born. She put cloth around Him and laid Him in a place where cattle are fed. There was no room for them in the place where people stay for the night.
LUKE 2:7 NLV

This verse hardly seems right. The family God chose to bring Jesus into the world couldn't find lodging space at an inn. So Mary and Joseph improvised, and Jesus was born in a stable. The new mother wrapped Jesus in a cloth and laid Him in a feed box for animals.

As an adult, Jesus' lodgings were still makeshift. He once said, "Foxes have holes. Birds have nests. But the Son of Man has no place to lay His head" (Matthew 8:20 NLV). He knew, however, that His mission wasn't about meeting His own needs. "The Son of Man did not come to be cared for," He said. "He came to care for others. He came to give His life so that many could be bought by His blood and be made free from sin" (Mark 10:45 NLV).

If you feel like you're lacking something important—money, talent, a girlfriend, whatever—follow Jesus' example. Reach out. Serve. Give. God will ultimately reward your obedience.

Lord, help me to be faithful even when I think I'm lacking.

What Happens to the Bad Guys?

"All who see you will leave you and say, 'Nineveh is destroyed! Who will have sorrow for her?' Where can I find anyone to comfort you?"

NAHUM 3:7 NLV

. . . .

If you want to live as a Christian in this world, you will suffer. That's the word from Jesus Himself: "In the world you will have much trouble" (John 16:33 NLV). But God will avenge the trouble others pour on you.

The Old Testament prophets warned Israel's enemies that they faced God's wrath for their misbehavior. Once in a while, those enemies repented, as Nineveh did under Jonah's preaching. But as you can see in Nahum's prophecy, the Ninevites were back under God's curse. Anyone who rejects His mercy will pay His very steep price.

In the New Testament, the apostle Paul wrote, "Do not be afraid of those who hate you. Their hate for you proves they will be destroyed. It proves you have life from God that lasts forever" (Philippians 1:28 NLV).

Don't let the bad guys get you down. You will be vindicated, when God punishes your enemies. . .or possibly makes them your brothers.

. . . .

Lord God, please turn our enemies into friends. Save the bad guys through Jesus' blood.

God Answers Prayer

*All the demons begged Him, saying, "Send us
into the swine, that we may enter into them."
And immediately Jesus gave them leave.*
MARK 5:12–13 SKJV

• •

Some people say that God always answers prayer—He
either says "yes," "no," or "wait." It can be frustrating
to be on the receiving end of a "no" or a "wait," but if
we believe that God is all-knowing, all-powerful, and
all-loving, we have to trust that His ways are best.

Today's scripture provides a strange encouragement for us. It shows Jesus—God in human flesh—giving *demons* what they asked for. If He was willing to do that, don't you think He'll fulfill your requests in the most appropriate time and way?

God is so far beyond us that He could engineer even the demons' request for His good purposes. The formerly possessed man was rid of his evil burden and immediately became a missionary to his own hometown. "All men marveled" (Mark 5:20 SKJV)—and some probably followed Jesus themselves.

God answers prayer. So pray!

• •

*Lord God, I thank You for Your wise and
helpful answers to prayer. Help me to be
patient when You say "no" or "wait."*

Misunderstood

For His brothers did not believe in Him.
JOHN 7:5 SKJV

Albert Einstein, one of the most famous intellectuals in history, had a less-than-glamorous beginning. When he was a child, his abstract musings confused his teachers, causing them to label him a poor student. The problem didn't lie with the child, though—it was in the adults' inability to recognize his genius.

Einstein's predicament echoes Jesus' life. He was God in human flesh, yet even some of His own family members thought he was insane (Mark 3:21). How humiliating that must have been! But Jesus didn't allow it to hinder His mission.

We all have times when we feel misunderstood and mistreated—maybe even because of our faith. The tension may come from family or friends, classmates, or coworkers.

During such times, remember this truth: the only approval you really need is God's. No matter what anyone else thinks, do what's right in the Lord's eyes—everything else will ultimately fall into place.

Father, it's hard to face opposition from the people around me. Give me the patience and strength to keep living for You.

God's Approval

Do you think I am trying to get the favor of men,
or of God? If I were still trying to please men,
I would not be a servant owned by Christ.
GALATIANS 1:10 NLV

∙∙

Before he was called Paul, Saul was "a Hebrew of the Hebrews" (Philippians 3:5 SKJV). He was present for the death of the first Christian martyr, collecting coats while others threw stones at Stephen. Saul defended his Jewish faith no matter what the cost. Then one day he met Jesus, and everything changed.

In Galatians, Paul wrote that if he were seeking the approval of men, he would never have become a Christian.

There is real tension between unbelievers and believers. Within that tension, we must always choose Christ, no matter the cost. Paul had a high social standing and many privileges that he abandoned for Jesus. Are we willing to give up everything for the Lord?

Jesus' teaching is "seek first the kingdom of God" (Matthew 6:33 SKJV). When we do that, we'll get everything we need in return.

∙∙

Father, create in me an obedient heart. Please remove
my desire for attention and approval from others.

Prepare for Trouble

*Others chose to be beaten instead of being set free,
because they would not turn against God. In this way,
they would be raised to a better life. Others were
talked against. Some were beaten. Some were put
in chains and in prison. They were killed by stones
being thrown at them. People were cut in pieces.
They were tested. They were killed with swords.*
HEBREWS 11:35–37 NLV

• •

It's not a pretty picture when the book of Hebrews describes the ways believers died for their faith rather than turn against God.

A *Christianity Today* article says that *seventy million* Christians have been killed for their faith since the time Jesus walked the earth. New York City has a population of about 8.5 million people, so imagine eight times that number of people martyred for Christ.

It's been generations since Western Christians have faced any such persecution. But, considering our culture's current trajectory, it could happen. Be ready, through Bible study, prayer, and the fellowship of strong Christian friends. Just know that, whatever the case, God will be faithful to see you through.

• •

*Lord Jesus, You died for me. Prepare me in
case I'm ever called to give my life for You.*

It'll Be Okay

He said, "Do not be afraid. You are looking for
Jesus of Nazareth Who was nailed to a cross. He is
risen! He is not here! See, here is the place where
they laid Him. Go and tell His followers and Peter
that He is going ahead of you into Galilee."
MARK 16:6–7 NLV

Can you imagine the heartache Peter must have felt after he betrayed Jesus? Put yourself in Peter's shoes: you boldly say you'll never leave Jesus' side, then just a day later deny even knowing Him. One day you draw a sword to protect your Messiah. Soon afterward you're frightened by a teen girl who says, "You were also with Jesus!" (Matthew 26:69 NLV).

Of course, Jesus knew everything that would happen with Peter—and how to make it right. That's why the angel in the empty tomb told Mary Magdalene and the other women to "tell His followers *and Peter*." When he heard their report, Peter must have known that everything would be okay.

The same goes for us. When we mess up, Jesus still loves us deeply. He's ready to forgive. Let's accept that forgiveness and move forward.

Jesus, please forgive my failures and
restore me to fellowship with You.

Canceled for Christ

*"If the world hates you, you know that
it hated Me before it hated you."*
JOHN 15:18 SKJV

. . . .

You've probably noticed an unfortunate trend: America (and the world in general) is treating Christianity more and more like the punchline to a joke.

As of the last several years, it's no longer popular to be a Christian who holds biblical values. Of course, you can still say Jesus' name, but the moment you start promoting what the Bible actually teaches, eyebrows go up and positive feelings go down.

But this reaction shouldn't surprise you. It's just what Jesus, who was eventually killed by the people who hated Him, said would happen.

Thankfully, most Christians today aren't at risk of being murdered for their faith—getting "canceled" by the in-crowd is the worst of it. . .for now, at least. But our response to this kind of pushback really matters. If we someday find ourselves in the lions' den, will we have developed enough backbone to stand strong? Or will we cave under the bigger pressures?

"Being canceled" may be simply a practice run. Are you passing God's test?

. . . .

*God, give me the courage to never
compromise Your truth.*

Hope When All Seems Lost

*"The Lord will fight for you. All you
have to do is keep still."*
EXODUS 14:14 NLV

• •

Ever felt like all hope was gone? That's exactly how the people of Israel felt, trapped between the Red Sea and the Egyptian army. But Moses told the people, "Do not be afraid! Be strong, and see how the Lord will save you today. For the Egyptians you have seen today, you will never see again" (Exodus 14:13 NLV).

God sometimes calls us to step out, to do something radical in order to grow our trust in Him. These times will be uncomfortable at best, maybe even terrifying.

When the Israelites took a step of faith, God made a way out of their predicament. They escaped across dry land and watched God wash their enemies away.

The victory won't always be as immediate or obvious, but God has a path forward for you too. He will fight for you. All you have to do is keep still.

• •

*Lord God, please help me to grow in my faith
and trust. With You, there is always hope.*

Leave It All Behind

*"I will go where you go. I will live where
you live. Your people will be my people.
And your God will be my God."*
RUTH 1:16 NLV

· ·

If you know the story of Ruth, you know that this young widow left her family, friends, and homeland behind to follow her mother-in-law, Naomi, to Bethlehem. Nothing Ruth had known in Moab could compare with her love for Naomi or her commitment to Naomi's God.

When we decide to follow Jesus, we make a similar break from our past. We certainly need to leave our sins behind. We may need to move on from old friends, activities, and interests. It's not that Jesus is the "fun police"—but He wants what is best for you, and He'll replace anything you give up with something better.

Leave your own "Moab" behind. You'll find your purpose and joy in "Bethlehem," among the people of God. Having left Moab, Ruth went on to become the great-grandmother of King David. What might God have in mind for *you* to accomplish?

· ·

Lord, give me the desire and strength to leave my old life behind. I want to do great things for Your kingdom.

Everything's Backwards!

*You have made the Lord tired with your words.
Yet you say, "How have we made Him tired?" By
saying, "Everyone who sins is good in the eyes
of the Lord, and He is pleased with them."*

MALACHI 2:17 NLV

• •

If you're not careful, you might start to think you're crazy for following Jesus.

Seriously. This world is so backwards that it calls sin good. Biblical righteousness is called evil. But that's nothing new.

Seven hundred years before Jesus was born, Isaiah wrote, "It is bad for those who call what is sinful good, and good sinful, who say dark is light and light is dark" (Isaiah 5:20 NLV). And four centuries before Christ, Malachi noted that his culture was saying, "Everyone who sins is good in the eyes of the Lord, and He is pleased with them"!

Of course, that wasn't true then and it isn't true now. No matter how backwards things get, you know the truth—the plain standards of God's Word. It's frustrating to live in an upside-down world, but God will give you strength. Just ask Him to keep you faithful.

• •

Lord, keep me true to Your perfect Word and ways.

It's Not Playtime

*Then Moses said to Aaron, "This is what the
Lord meant when He said, 'I will show Myself
holy among those who are near Me. I will
be honored in front of all the people.'"*
LEVITICUS 10:3 NLV

Nadab and Abihu, the sons of Aaron the priest, messed up big time. Leviticus 10 describes how they took an offering to God that the Lord had not commanded. Not only that, they went into the "most holy place" of the tabernacle without invitation. God was so offended that He sent a fire that burned the two men to death.

It's a troubling story, to be sure. But we must remember that God cannot associate with anything that is unholy. The offering of Nadab and Abihu wasn't holy, and neither were they.

What does this mean for us? We should never trifle with God. Through His death on the cross, Jesus has made us holy in the eyes of the Lord. But that doesn't mean it's playtime—there are still consequences for sin. Let's be grateful for the work Jesus did on our behalf, and make sure we never intentionally do what God forbids. Really, why should we even want to?

*Lord, I thank You for Your forgiveness.
Help me to live for You!*

Obsolete Shame

*The Father. . .has made us suitable to be partakers
of the inheritance of the saints in light.*
COLOSSIANS 1:12 SKJV

• •

I'm not worthy.

Without a doubt, at some point, every Christian has thought those words.

While it's true that none of us are worthy of God's kindness, that's not the issue anymore. When He looks at you, God doesn't see the sins you've committed, the shame you feel, or the past you're trying to escape. He sees the righteousness of Jesus, who took the punishment that you (and everyone else) deserved.

One big mistake Christians fall into is dwelling on past errors. Doing so defeats the purpose of God's grace—it basically tells Him, "Thanks, but Your mercy isn't good enough. I'm still guilty."

And that's not all that obsessing over out-of-date guilt does. It can slowly poison your soul, transforming a peaceful mind into a wasteland of fear and depression.

Thankfully, God's plan is so much better. Today, consciously give your guilt to God—and watch Him replace it with His love. Shame is obsolete—freedom is now in fashion!

• •

*Thank You, Lord, for accepting me despite my failures.
May I release the sin and guilt that You died to destroy.*

Never Give Up

*While praying to God our Father, we always remember
your work of faith and your acts of love and your
hope that never gives up in our Lord Jesus Christ.*
1 THESSALONIANS 1:3 NLV

. . . .

Frodo Baggins is the small, unlikely hero of *The Lord of
the Rings*. He has no magical powers, and he's certainly
not a strong warrior. But Frodo is willing to traverse
enemy territory, carrying the "ring of power" while
withstanding its temptations, and throw the trouble-
some object into the burning heart of Mount Doom.
Through terrible struggle, Frodo never gives up.

In his letter to the Thessalonian church, the apostle
Paul specifically mentions their "hope that never gives
up." Perseverance is a key aspect of the Christian life
(see Romans 5:3–4; 2 Thessalonians 3:5; Hebrews 12:1;
James 1:3–4; 2 Peter 1:5–6). Not giving up is a choice—
you don't have to be strong or perfect or anything but
committed. And God will help you if you ask.

If you find yourself discouraged today, keep moving
forward. Seek our Christian friends, read scripture,
pray. These things will build a hope that never ends.

. . . .

*Father, create in me a hope that burns brightly. Provide
friendships and encouragement on my faith journey.*

Love, Respect, Honor

*Grandchildren are the pride and joy of old
men and a son is proud of his father.*
PROVERBS 17:6 NLV

. . . .

Do your parents or grandparents ever embarrass you?
Do they seem old and out of touch with your world?

You might not believe this now, but the time will
come when your music, movies, clothes, and hairstyles
will be completely out of fashion. In fact, younger
generations will laugh at how uncool *you* were!

Your parents and grandparents might not be able
to relate to what you enjoy, and vice versa. But that
doesn't change the fact that they love you and have a
lot of hard-earned wisdom to share. Don't let their lack
of the "cool factor" interfere with your relationship.
God put you in your family for a reason—and His plan
is that you learn from the older generations.

Along the way, be sure to love, respect, and honor
your parents and grandparents. It's the right thing to
do biblically. . .and someday, sooner than you can ever
imagine, *you'll* be the older generation. Then you'll
understand exactly why God has set things up as He has.

. . . .

*Lord, I thank You for my family. Please help
me to honor my parents and grandparents
as You would have me do.*

I Will Wait for You

I did not give up waiting for the Lord.
And He turned to me and heard my cry.
PSALM 40:1 NLV

• •

"Patience is a virtue." You've probably heard the phrase at least once in your life. In Psalm 40, David described how the Lord saved him from danger, placed him on safe ground, and put joy in his heart. But David had a job to do: "I did not give up waiting for the Lord."

Have you ever been impatient? That typically leads to frustration, a bad attitude, and disappointment. Impatience can even hurt those around us. So, what's the point? If all impatience creates is negativity, why not work at being patient?

Patience is more than a virtue. It's a gift from God, and it takes practice! Every morning as you wake up, ask the Lord to give you the energy and will to practice patience. You won't do it perfectly—but over time, you'll do better and better. You'll find that living a patient life produces much joy in your heart.

• •

Lord, give me the ability to be patient with the
people and situations I encounter today.

Haman's Mistake

And when Haman saw that Mordecai did not bow or show him reverence, then Haman was full of anger.
ESTHER 3:5 SKJV

. . . .

If you're looking for a suitable comparison to Haman, consider the school bully.

We all know that when life gets hard, our insecurities can take root. And what's an easy way to deal with our own insecurities? How about making life harder on others to feel like we're in control? Clearly, though, that's not the right way to deal with our frustrations.

Nobody likes a bully—not even the bully himself. Even if he gets a temporary thrill from hurting someone else, there comes a time when the bully realizes how sad and empty he is.

Fortunately, God offers us all a way out. We don't have to dominate others to feel validated—we can find our true purpose by surrendering our lives to the Lord. When we release our desire for control, God can truly work in our lives. As James wrote, "Humble yourselves in the sight of the Lord, and He shall lift you up" (4:10 SKJV).

. . . .

Father, I don't want to be like Haman. Please use my insecurities to draw me closer to You.

You're in Good Company

*"Blessed are you when men revile you and
persecute you, and say all manner of evil
against you falsely for My sake."*
MATTHEW 5:11 SKJV

• •

Have you ever been mistreated for being a Christian?
Did a friend avoid you, a teacher call you out in class,
or a coach belittle you in front of your teammates?

Jesus' solution is this: "Rejoice and be exceed-
ingly glad, for great is your reward in heaven, for so
they persecuted the prophets who were before you"
(Matthew 5:12 SKJV). Our Lord doesn't call us to wallow
in pity, but to be happy and thankful! Why? Because
poor treatment is exactly what the world gives to
followers of Jesus—and you are being recognized as
one of them.

The unsaved world hates believers who resem-
ble their Lord. If you're facing trouble for your faith,
you're in good company. Stay the course, knowing
you've been marked by others as a prince in God's
kingdom.

• •

*Lord, help me to remember that when others treat
me poorly for my faith, I am part of a brotherhood,
the true believers deeply devoted to You.*

Don't Lose Hope

I wept much, because no man was found worthy to open and to read the book, or to look in it. And one of the elders said to me, "Do not weep. Behold, the Lion of the tribe of Judah, the Root of David, has prevailed to open the book and to open its seven seals."
REVELATION 5:4–5 SKJV

• •

Two thousand years ago, John was given a glimpse into heaven. He saw God the Father holding a book representing His purposes for mankind. The book was sealed, and an angel called out, "Who is worthy to open the book?" (Revelation 5:2 SKJV). No one was found.

Feeling hopeless, John began to weep. But then he was told that Jesus had arrived to open the book. The news caused all of heaven to break out in worship.

You will face challenges that seem impossible to overcome. But Jesus is always able: "By Him all things were created that are in heaven and that are on earth, visible and invisible. . . . All things were created by Him and for Him. And He is before all things, and by Him all things consist" (Colossians 1:16–17 SKJV).

Don't lose hope! Jesus can handle anything that troubles you.

• •

Lord God, help me to take my eyes off my challenges and fix them on Christ.

God Is Just

*The Lord says, "For three sins of Damascus and
for four, I will not hold back punishment."*
AMOS 1:3 NLV

It's tough to see just how wicked our world is. Seemingly every day, the dishonesty and corruption and violence increase. Sometimes we only view the trouble on our screens. At other times, people's sin touches us and our loved ones personally. This broken, messed-up world makes our individual lives harder all the time.

If you ever feel overwhelmed by the injustice, know that God doesn't. He is fully aware of who's suffering and who's causing the trouble. And He has a plan to make everything right. Those of us who truly follow Jesus will be rewarded with rest. The troublemakers will be punished. In Amos 1, Damascus, Philistia, Tyre, Edom, and Ammon all heard the same pronouncement of judgment: "For three sins. . .and for four, I will not hold back punishment" (verses 3, 6, 9, 11, and 13).

God is just. He will ultimately take care of everything—including you.

*Lord God, it's hard to see people hurting
other people. Please protect those who are
suffering, and speed Your justice for all.*

Who Do You Follow?

Do not trouble yourself because of sinful men.
Do not want to be like those who do wrong.
PSALM 37:1 NLV

. . . .

Take a minute and think about the friends you hang out with. When people see you with them, would they say that you're trying to reflect Jesus? If you can't honestly answer yes, maybe it's time to hang out with a different crowd.

The psalm writer wasn't saying we can't spend time with lost people. He was telling us not to *live* like lost people. If our desire is to do the same things that the unsaved are doing, our desire clearly isn't to do the things Jesus has called us to.

Let's be very careful not only of our peers, but of the actors, athletes, and influencers we follow. If their behavior doesn't reflect the life of Jesus, steer clear.

. . . .

Lord Jesus, please give me wisdom to choose
the right people to follow. Ultimately, help
me to model Yourself most of all.

Compromised

*"Therefore, come out from among them
and be separate," says the Lord.*
2 Corinthians 6:17 skjv

• •

In politics, compromise is a key to ending disagreements. It's a sign of fairmindedness and understanding, and it has resolved many a conflict.

But Christianity is not just a branch of politics. It's a living relationship with the God of the universe—not something you want to treat lightly.

As a result, compromising on God's laws is simply not an option. "Meeting halfway" to make others happy is tantamount to saying, "Yeah, God's important. . .but He's not *that* important." As Paul wrote just a couple of verses before today's reading, "What agreement does Christ have with Belial [Satan]? Or what part does he who believes have with an unbeliever?" (2 Corinthians 6:15 skjv).

It's hard to maintain an unpopular opinion. In fact, many Christians have died for that. But God promises a reward far greater than we can even imagine— definitely better than any human praise we'll get for compromising.

• •

*You went far enough to die for me, Jesus—so help me
never to compromise when it comes to honoring You.*

Wait for Him

*David became greater and greater, for
the Lord God of All was with him.*
2 SAMUEL 5:10 NLV

• •

Have you ever felt overwhelmed by school, friendships, or life in general? Sometimes, everywhere you look seems dark. David occasionally felt that way. He was anointed as king—but while another king was on the throne. Saul was homicidally jealous of his position and set David on the run. He had to beg for food, live in caves, even pretend he was insane to survive. Can you imagine?

Out of this chaos, though, David called out to God. The stressed-out young man put his hope in the Lord. As David wrote in Psalm 130:5 (NLV), "I wait for the Lord. My soul waits and I hope in His Word."

No matter how hard things got, David believed what God had promised. In the end, Saul would be removed from the throne and David crowned as his replacement. The Lord God of All was always with David, just as He is with you.

• •

*Father, I wait patiently to see You. Please
show up in my life to tame the chaos.*

Persecution Is an Opportunity

"But before all this happens, men will take hold of you and make it very hard for you. They will give you over to the places of worship and to the prisons. They will bring you in front of kings and the leaders of the people. This will all be done to you because of Me."
LUKE 21:12 NLV

• •

In Luke 21, Jesus' disciples discussed the majesty of the temple in Jerusalem. But the Lord quickly told them the temple would soon be destroyed and His followers would face terrible persecution. This was no reason for fear, however.

Jesus actually saw these things as opportunities for believers to advance the gospel. "This will be a time for you to tell about Me. Do not think about what you will say ahead of time. For I will give you wisdom in what to say and I will help you say it. Those who are against you will not be able to stop you or say you are wrong" (Luke 21:13–15 NLV).

Our culture is increasingly hostile to Jesus and those who follow Him. But that's really an opportunity to tell persecutors about your Lord.

• •

Lord, give me courage to stand up and speak for You.

When Others Fight Dirty

"And it has been found that the city has turned against kings in past times, and that plans against kings have been made in it. . . ." Then the work on the house of God in Jerusalem stopped.
EZRA 4:19, 24 NLV

. . . .

All through history, there have been men and women who fought for the betterment of humanity. But in every fight for good, you'll also see evil fighting dirty. At some point in your own endeavor for righteousness, you'll probably face some dirty tactics from people around you. You'll definitely hear from Satan himself, attacking your mind with thoughts of doubt and regret.

The enemy will try to distract you from the truth that Jesus set you free from your sins and failures. But when Satan starts fighting dirty, just remember that you're on the winning side. Deuteronomy 20:4 (NLV) says, "The Lord your God is the One Who goes with you. He will fight for you against those who hate you. And He will save you."

This life is warfare. Be ready for difficulties and reverses. But know that God ultimately wins—and you will win with Him. Just stay close to His side.

. . . .

Father, help me to withstand the enemy's attacks. Remind me that You have already won the war!

It's for God's Glory

Jesus. . .said, "This sickness is not to death,
but for the glory of God, that the Son
of God might be glorified by it."
JOHN 11:4 SKJV

Lazarus was dead. His body had been in the tomb four days, and the smelly decomposition process was underway. Nothing could be done. All hope was lost.

Except Jesus didn't see it that way.

Standing before the tomb, He spoke three simple words—"Lazarus, come out!" (John 11:43 SKJV). The silence was broken by a rustling. Soon, a man wrapped in cloths, looking like something out of the movie *The Mummy*, came shuffling out. Lazarus was alive, and "many of the Jews who. . .had seen the things that Jesus did believed in Him" (John 11:45 SKJV).

That's the great takeaway of the story of Lazarus—and of much of the hardship we face. When Jesus works in and through us, He and His Father are glorified. In every frustration and trial and tragedy—if we maintain focus on our Lord—we'll begin to understand how everything combines to fulfill God's master plan.

Our ongoing story is building toward a grand resolution that will be "for the glory of God."

Lord, help me see that nothing, not
even death, can stop Your plans.

Exceptions to the Rule

Joash was seven years old when he became king. And he ruled forty years in Jerusalem.
2 Chronicles 24:1 NLV

• •

Would you like to be called too short? How about too slow? Or would you want to hear that you just don't have what it takes? Martin St. Louis heard all those gripes. He had talent for ice hockey, but he was told he would never make it to the NHL.

In his Hall of Fame acceptance speech, though, St. Louis said that when people tried to discourage him, it was simply motivation to work harder. Over his professional hockey career, he'd scored more than a thousand points and won a Stanley Cup, among other achievements. He persevered and proved his doubters wrong.

The biblical Joash was only seven when he became king. No doubt he had doubters! But he succeeded when he followed the Lord. That's something any of us can do. No matter what others say about you, follow God, work hard. . .and prove the doubters wrong.

• •

Lord, help me to turn others' doubts into fuel to persevere. Your opinion is the only one that truly matters!

Power through Faith

*Every child of God has power over the sins
of the world. The way we have power over
the sins of the world is by our faith.*
1 JOHN 5:4 NLV

∙∙∙

Have you struggled with a sin that just seems too hard
to beat? No doubt, our temptations are strong. Our
bodies want pleasure, and they don't really care what
we believe. And, of course, Satan is pushing you to
give in—to do the wrong thing and sin against God.
But as a follower of Jesus, a child of God, you have
the power to defeat sin.

How? Through faith. Faith that believes Jesus is
stronger than your feelings. Faith that believes God
will make a way for you to avoid sin when temptation
comes (1 Corinthians 10:13). Faith that leaves "Egypt"
behind, walking away on dry ground where the Red
Sea lay just moments before.

Faith is a gift from God, but we make it stronger
by exercise. Take a scripture like today's and speak it
when temptation comes. This creates a "virtuous circle"
of increasing ability to say no to sin.

∙∙∙

*Lord, I want this kind of faith. I want to put my
faith in action, to overcome my sin for Your glory.*

Stand Strong, Together

"Our God whom we serve is able to deliver us from the burning fiery furnace. And He will deliver us out of your hand, O king. But if not, let it be known to you, O king, that we will not serve your gods, nor worship the golden statue that you have set up."
DANIEL 3:17–18 SKJV

Shadrach, Meshach, and Abednego are almost a Christian cliché. We know their story so well, we're tempted to breeze right past it.

Don't. God wrote them into scripture so we could gain from their example. These Jewish friends, living in a hostile Babylonian culture, stood up for God—literally. When everyone else bowed before Nebuchadnezzar's golden statue, Shadrach, Meshach, and Abednego stood tall.

You probably know that they were punished. But God made sure the fiery furnace had no effect on them whatsoever. When we honor Him, He honors us.

It's a lot easier to stand for God when you have support. Take it from Shadrach, Meshach, and Abednego: a quality friend makes hard times easier. If you don't have that kind of friend now, ask God to send one your way.

Father, please help me to find—and be—the kind of friend Shadrach, Meshach, and Abednego were.

Confidence in God

The Lord sat as King over the flood.
The Lord sits as King forever.
PSALM 29:10 NLV

• •

You probably know the story of Noah and the ark. If not, here's the short version: God was weary of people's sin and decided to destroy the earth with a flood to start over. He told Noah to build a giant boat, big enough to hold two of every creature that walked on land. Everyone else probably thought Noah was crazy, but he wasn't—God did exactly what He'd planned, wiping out all humanity except for Noah and his family.

Throughout the ark-building and the flood itself, Noah must have had questions and even fears. But he trusted the Lord, knowing that God was in control.

That is still true for us today. No matter how out of control your circumstances may feel, God has everything in hand. You can be sure that He will never lose His grip or give up on you! God sits as King over the flood. He sits as King over whatever storm you're going through.

• •

Heavenly Father, help me to remember that You're
in control even when I'm tempted to think otherwise.
Help me to put my trust in You no matter what.

Joy in Pain

We are troubled on every side, yet not
distressed. . .always bearing about in the body
the dying of the Lord Jesus, that the life of Jesus
might also be made evident in our body.
2 CORINTHIANS 4:8, 10 SKJV

• •

Standing up for your faith can be hard. For some people—such as the apostle Paul—"hard" means being conspired against, arrested, beaten, imprisoned, and even stoned on a semi-regular basis. For most of us, however, it simply means going against the flow.

But don't let the distance between these two extremes fool you—hard is still hard, no matter what form it takes. When that guy in the cafeteria is laughing at you for praying over your lunch, the pressure is just as real as if someone were chucking rocks at you.

Through the Spirit's help, Paul mastered the art of being unfazed in disaster. In fact, he was even *consoled* by the pain, knowing that he was following his Savior's example.

The next time you face persecution, remember that Jesus knows exactly how you feel—and that He's cheering every step you take.

• •

Thank You, Lord, for paying the ultimate
price for my salvation. Help me to stand
up for You, no matter what the cost.

Community

Day after day they went to the house of God together. In their houses they ate their food together. Their hearts were happy. They gave thanks to God and all the people respected them. The Lord added to the group each day those who were being saved from the punishment of sin.
ACTS 2:46–47 NLV

. . . .

When a team wins a championship, the coach will say things like "We stuck together" or "Everyone bought in and contributed to our success." Teamwork, not a single person, was the reason for the victory.

That kind of community effort made the early church successful. They shared meals and encouraged one another. The provided for each other's physical needs. They prayed.

If you're not "winning" in your spiritual life, seek out the Christian community. Find mature believers who will share a meal with you, encourage you, pray for you. Remember Ecclesiastes 4:12 (NLV): "One man is able to have power over him who is alone, but two can stand against him."

Your faith journey was always meant to be traveled with other believers. Stay connected. Be encouraged. Grow.

. . . .

Lord, I thank you for other believers. Please lead me to those who will help me in my journey.

Faith in Action

When the child was grown, he went out one day to his father who was with those gathering grain. He said to his father, "O, my head, my head!" The father said to his servant, "Carry him to his mother."
2 KINGS 4:18–19 NLV

• •

God is far beyond our understanding. A woman in a town called Shunem found that out when her son died.

This woman pursued Elisha, the prophet who sometimes stayed in her family's home. He agreed to return to her place, where he found the boy dead. But Elisha prayed, and God restored the child's life.

You may think this is a far-fetched example—that God isn't raising people from the dead these days. But that's not really the point. This boy's mother believed God for something big. She put her faith in action and sought out a prophet to help.

At times, we all face big, tough things, whether health problems, strained relationships, or financial issues. Like the woman of Shunem, you can reach out for help too—from praying friends and from God Himself. He may or may not resolve your issue in the way you hope. But you can be sure that His ways are always best.

• •

Lord, I trust You with my life. You will use Your complete knowledge for my best interests.

Lost in the Dark

Your word is a lamp to my feet and a light to my path.
PSALM 119:105 SKJV

• •

Have you ever gotten lost? Have you ever gotten lost *at night*? It's way worse to be lost when you don't have natural light to help you identify landmarks and signs.

When times get tough, it's like you're lost in the dark. You may seek out answers from the wrong people. You may begin to question God's existence. You may be tempted to escape into sin. That's why God's Word is so important—it is the light for your path.

Imagine the Bible as a good, working flashlight in the junk drawer. When the power goes out, that flashlight will be a big help around your darkened house. . .but only if you take it out of the drawer and use it. In the same way, an unread Bible on your shelf does no good at all.

Reading devotionals is a good start. But why not spend some extra time today in God's Word? It's truly a lamp to your feet.

• •

Lord God, please light up the darkness in
my life. Help me to see the path You've laid
out for me. I want to walk in Your light!

Friends in Need. . .

*Two are better than one, because they have
a good reward for their labor. For if they
fall, the one will lift up his companion.*
ECCLESIASTES 4:9 SKJV

Near the end of the *Lord of the Rings* movie trilogy, Frodo Baggins struggles to finish his mission—to carry the "ring of power" to Mount Doom and destroy it once and for all. The ring, symbolic of sin and power and greed, corrupts and twists all who wield it—and Frodo is no exception. But when he collapses onto the burnt, rocky ground, unable to take another step, Frodo's trusted companion, Samwise Gamgee, speaks the immortal line: "I can't carry it for you, but I can carry *you*." Samwise then picks up Frodo and begins trudging toward their fiery destination.

What a depiction of today's scripture! We all have a "ring" we must bear, and we can't do it alone. That's why God sends friends to help and counsel us when we stumble. It's our responsibility to accept such help as it comes. . .and offer it when we see our own friends in need.

*God, thank You for the friends You've sent
my way. Help me encourage them in their
Christian walk, just as they encourage me.*

Do It God's Way

"When you hear the long sound of the ram's horn, all the people should call out with a loud noise. The wall of the city will fall to the ground. And then all the people will all go in the city."

JOSHUA 6:5 NLV

It's getting tougher and tougher to be a Christian in this culture. Hostility to true biblical faith is growing in both quantity and intensity. Followers of Jesus may be tempted to cut corners spiritually to try to keep the mob off their backs.

But God's ways are always best. Thousands of years ago, the Lord gave Joshua a strange battle plan for defeating the powerful city of Jericho: Walk around the place several times. Blow trumpets and shout. The walls will collapse, and you'll be able to walk right in.

Seriously, God? Yes—Joshua did what God said and enjoyed great success.

We will too as we do things God's way. That's not to say our lives will be easy. But God definitely rewards those who serve Him faithfully. (Check out Jesus' parable in Luke 19:11–28.)

Lord God, help me always to do things Your way. I want to obey You to the letter.

Bloom Where You're Planted

In the days when there were judges to rule, there was a time of no food in the land. A certain man of Bethlehem in Judah went to visit the land of Moab with his wife and his two sons.
RUTH 1:1 NLV

• •

Parents often have to make difficult decisions. Maybe your parents have made a choice that affected you big time. If so, you can relate to the two sons in this story: Mahlon and Chilion.

Their parents, Elimelech and Naomi, left Bethlehem during a famine. They went to live in Moab, a place that seemed to have more food. Mahlon and Chilion probably didn't have a say in the matter. But a family has to eat, right? Even so, the move was probably tough for the two boys who had to start over in an unfamiliar culture.

When your parents make decisions you don't like, keep in mind that they're trying to satisfy everyone's best interests. You can help by praying and trusting God to come through for all of you.

• •

Lord, I want to honor my father or mother even when I don't agree with or understand their decisions. I thank You for creating parents to love and care for their children.

You *Can* Do What You *Need* to Do

Then I said, "O, Lord God! I do not know
how to speak. I am only a boy."
JEREMIAH 1:6 NLV

• •

The teen years are tricky. People are expecting more and more from you but you don't yet enjoy full adult freedom. Sometimes older people are holding you back. Other times you limit yourself.

When God called Jeremiah to be a prophet, the young man responded by saying, "I am only a boy." God's response? "Do not say, 'I am only a boy.' You must go everywhere I send you. And you must say whatever I tell you. Do not be afraid of them. For I am with you to take you out of trouble" (Jeremiah 1:7–8 NLV).

Jeremiah *could* do whatever he *needed* to do—in God's strength. That's true of every Christian guy. Whether you're thinking, like Jeremiah, "I'm too young," or someone else has imposed that label on you, pray for God's wisdom and leading. He'll give you everything you need at the moment you need it. Just allow Him to work.

• •

Lord, I want to live out Your plan, in Your way, in
Your time. Give me patience, wisdom, and courage.

Faith and Time

And it came to pass after these things,
that God tested Abraham.
GENESIS 22:1 SKJV

• •

We've heard the story of Abraham and Isaac a hundred times—and know the whole thing was simply a test. Still, it's hard not to tense up as we reach the part when Abraham raises the knife, resolved to follow God's command to kill his only son.

Abraham was only a man, no different than any of us. Just as we sometimes wonder about God's over-arching plan, Abraham struggled with his own questions and doubts. What set him apart from the rest of us is the enormity of his trust in God.

The Lord knows each of our weaknesses. He also knows exactly how much we can take. Often, He gives us a load beyond what we think we can handle, requiring us to turn to Him for strength. That's way Abraham told Isaac, "God will provide Himself a lamb for a burnt offering" (Genesis 22:8 SKJV).

When soul-crushing trials arise, remember that God will provide a solution. You just need faith and a little more time.

• •

Lord, You've designed the tests of life to
bring me closer to You. Grant me the faith
to overcome and bring You all the glory.

Do Your Duty

The spring of the year was the time when kings went out to battle. At that time David sent Joab and his servants and all Israel. They destroyed the sons of Ammon and gathered the army around Rabbah. But David stayed at Jerusalem.

2 Samuel 11:1 NLV

Today's scripture describes the beginning of David's darkest hours. Instead of doing what kings typically did, David kicked back and let others go off to war. While there's nothing wrong with delegating jobs, David wasn't busy with something else. While he idled, sin took hold and disaster struck.

In life there are always chances to dodge the important thing we really should be doing. But God calls us to action, not idleness. The lazy David noticed a beautiful neighbor, sent men to bring her to him, and committed adultery with her. Then he had the woman's husband—one of his best, most loyal soldiers—killed.

When you feel the temptation to cut corners, think about King David—the "man after God's own heart" who really made a mess of things. Never let your guard down. Always do your duty.

Father in heaven, please empower me to do what You have called me to do—every time.

The Anchor

We who have turned to Him can have great comfort
knowing that He will do what He has promised. This
hope is a safe anchor for our souls. It will never move.
HEBREWS 6:18–19 NLV

• •

It's bound to happen at some point: someone is going to
break a promise to you. People are imperfect and often
self-serving. The good news is that God will always do
what He promised. He is a safe anchor for our souls.

What has God promised you? Here are just a few
examples: "I will never leave you or let you be alone"
(Hebrews 13:5 NLV). Jesus said, "For sure, I tell you,
anyone who hears My Word and puts his trust in Him
Who sent Me has life that lasts forever. He will not be
guilty. He has already passed from death into life" (John
5:24 NLV). The apostle Paul wrote, "My God will give
you everything you need because of His great riches
in Christ Jesus" (Philippians 4:19 NLV).

In a world of broken promises, God shines as a
beacon of truth. You can trust Him to be an anchor
for your soul.

• •

Lord, I trust Your promises.
They are a great comfort to me.

God's Strange Nudges

Ananias said, "But Lord, many people have told me about this man. He is the reason many of Your followers in Jerusalem have had to suffer much."
ACTS 9:13 NLV

• •

Have you ever felt like God was nudging you to do something, but it didn't make sense? Ananias knew exactly how that feels.

In the early days of the church, Christians were being punished for following Jesus. Stephen had just been martyred. A rabid Pharisee named Saul wanted to throw every Christian he found into prison.

In Damascus, Ananias heard God say, "Get up! Go over to Straight Street to Judas' house and ask for a man from the city of Tarsus. His name is Saul. You will find him praying there" (Acts 9:11 NLV). Ananias didn't yet know that God had already dealt with Saul in a dramatic way. All Ananias could think was, *That's the man who wants to persecute me!*

Ananias protested briefly—but obeyed when God again said, "Go!" (Acts 9:15). And he helped start a new believer on a path that would literally change the world.

Don't dismiss those strange nudges from God. He may be planning something amazing.

• •

Lord God, give me the courage to obey You, even when things don't make sense to me.

Forgive Your Enemy

*If you count me therefore a partner, receive him
as myself. If he has wronged you or owes you
anything, put that on my account. I, Paul, have
written it with my own hand: I will repay it.*
Philemon 17–19 skjv

• •

Forgiving a person who's done you wrong can be one
of the hardest choices you will ever make. People are
flawed and make mistakes—lots of them—so there's
no doubt that someday you will face the choice to
forgive. That's exactly what the apostle Paul was asking
Philemon to do.

Philemon had owned a slave named Onesimus.
Apparently, he stole from Philemon and ran away. But
God providentially brought Onesimus into contact with
Paul and a relationship with Jesus Christ. Paul wanted
to send Onesimus right back to the people he'd stolen
from to help spread the gospel.

So Paul asked Philemon to forgive Onesimus. But
the apostle took things one step further by offering to
repay any debt Onesimus owed. How Christlike Paul's
offer. It's an example we are all called to follow.

• •

*Jesus, help me to forgive others
because You have forgiven me.*

Fear of Missing Out

For what is your life? It is even a vapor, that
appears for a little time and then vanishes away.
JAMES 4:14 SKJV

Want to know about a friend's vacation? Social media's got you covered. Want to see what Congress is up to? Scores of news sites are available. Want to research any of a thousand complex subjects? A quick search and a few minutes of scrolling will do the trick.

We live in the information age. But this constant flow of data has produced a strange side effect: FOMO, the fear of missing out.

The stress of FOMO is closely related to the truth of today's scripture: life is short. Since every day contains but twenty-four hours—unchanged since the creation—it's inevitable that you'll find yourself "not up to speed" on some topic.

Fortunately, Christians have no need to worry. It's okay if some things slip under your radar—after all, none of this really matters in the long term. The Bible is clear regarding the true meaning of life: "Fear God and keep His commandments" (Ecclesiastes 12:13 SKJV).

Now there's a truth you don't want to miss out on.

Lord, please banish FOMO from my life—
as long as I have You, I'll be satisfied.

Tough Decisions Require Good Advice

Rehoboam said to them, "Come to me again in three days." So the people left.
2 Chronicles 10:5 NLV

• •

When King Solomon died, his son Rehoboam took power. Shortly after ascending to the throne, the new king was approached by the people of Israel. They wanted a break from Solomon's heavy expectations of work and taxes. The people promised faithful service if Rehoboam would just lighten their load.

Rehoboam sought advice, which was a good idea. First, he went to the elders who had served his father. They recommended a reprieve. But then Rehoboam consulted with the young men who'd grown up with him. They wanted to make the people work even harder.

Unfortunately, the new king listened to the younger men. He insulted his people and caused his own kingdom to split in two.

When you have an important decision to make, seek out the best advice. Don't just invite your peers' thoughts—look for older, and potentially wiser, men as well. Be sure the ones you listen to are those who know and fear God.

• •

Father, be with me in my decision making. Help me to be wise and to seek Your ways.

Poor and Happy

*"Those of you who are poor are happy,
because the holy nation of God is yours."*
LUKE 6:20 NLV

• •

Seventy or eighty years of life on earth are short in comparison to eternity. But many people focus a big chunk of their lives on building wealth, trying to ensure they have "enough" for when they're older.

The Bible does call us as Christians to work hard and pay our own way. It even encourages people to leave an inheritance to their children's children. But when money becomes our focus, we'll never be content.

In today's scripture, Jesus points out that those who are poor are happy. What He meant was that poor believers—whether poor in finances or in spirit—can be satisfied because they have a rich eternity ahead.

This world will urge you to chase after wealth, though that rarely if ever ends well. With a biblical view of money, though, you can find happiness and contentment, no matter how much you have.

• •

*Lord God, keep me from falling for the world's
lies about money. It will never satisfy—
but eternity with You certainly will.*

Watch, Pray, Win

But Jonah ran away from the Lord.
JONAH 1:3 NLV

• •

What's the story of Jonah really about? That you should always wear a life jacket? Nah. That you should always obey God? Ultimately, yes. But there's a related lesson in this brief Old Testament book: the need to fight temptation in our lives.

God gave Jonah a clear command. Jonah immediately wanted to disobey. Ever have that feeling yourself? Everyone does. And though it isn't easy to overcome our temptations, it isn't impossible either—as long as we rely on God's strength. Notice what the apostle Paul said about temptation in 1 Corinthians 10:13 (NLV): "God is faithful. He will not allow you to be tempted more than you can take. But when you are tempted, *He will make a way for you to keep from falling into sin*" (emphasis added because that's your big takeaway!).

How can you find that way out? Jesus said, "Watch and pray so that you will not be tempted" (Mark 14:38 NLV). No special skill required, just willingness. Can you commit to watching and praying today?

• •

Lord, I don't want temptation to trap me. Give me the wisdom and will to watch, pray, and win.

Don't Be Hasty

*"If a person without thinking swears he will
do something, whether bad or good, any
foolish promise a person may swear, when
he learns about it, he will be guilty."*
LEVITICUS 5:4 NLV

Ever made a promise you weren't sure you could keep? It can be hard to say no, and sometimes we rush into commitments that we don't have the time or ability to do. Unfortunately, broken promises make every situation more difficult, and they're actually sinful.

Jesus told us, simply, "Let your yes be YES. Let your no be NO" (Matthew 5:37 NLV). Sometimes it's hard to turn people down, but that can be a healthy practice—even at times when the opportunities are good. Learn to identify the things that are necessary and the things that can wait. Then slow down, take a few deep breaths, and carefully consider what you're about to commit to.

Be honest with yourself and others. If you say yes, keep your word. If you say no, be watching for other, better things on which to spend your time.

*Lord God, help me not to make hasty decisions.
I want to uphold the commitments I make. Give me
discernment to say no to whatever is not right for me.*

Spiritual Reprogramming

From where do wars and fighting come among you? Do they not come from here: even of your lusts that war in your members?
JAMES 4:1 SKJV

• •

Humans are wired for conflict. When we perceive a threat to our safety or superiority, our muscles tense, our hearts beat faster, and our adrenaline prepares us for combat.

This can be useful when a rabid dog attacks—but what about when two siblings disagree over what movie to watch? We all must learn to control our impulses and exercise patience.

Sadly, a lot of Christians struggle with this. Many of our lives are consumed by jealousy and pettiness. Most of the time, we don't lash out physically—but the words we speak in moments of anger can cause more lasting damage than a black eye will.

The everyday stresses of life can run our patience thin—that's why we need God to help us out. He's the only one who can remove our selfishness and replace it with His love.

• •

Lord God, please rid me of my angry, reactionary impulses. Show me how to resolve conflicts with grace and love.

An Heir

So now you are no longer a servant who is owned by someone. You are a son. If you are a son, then you will receive what God has promised through Christ.
GALATIANS 4:7 NLV

Imagine that your father is a multibillionaire. You've grown up with the best food, cars, clothes, houses, and opportunities this world can provide. But then you graduate high school, leave home, and live in an old VW van. You never take advantage of your incredible family connection.

Who would do that? Well, we as Christians, sometimes. We actually forget who we are in Christ. We're not just followers of Jesus; we're actually sons of God, heirs of the King. And to God, a multibillionaire is poor. The Lord owns the entire universe.

Today, remind yourself of just who you are—an heir of God who will receive all He has promised through Jesus Christ. So junk that old VW van. . .your mansion awaits.

*Father, help me always to remember that
I am a prince in Your kingdom.*

Don't Be Surprised

*Do not be surprised if the world
hates you, Christian brothers.*
1 JOHN 3:13 NLV

• •

When you live the Christian life the way God intends, people who don't share your faith will probably oppose you. Oh, they might give you a thumbs-up for helping the needy—but when you refuse to participate in their sin, the unsaved will turn on you quickly.

Don't be surprised by that. Jesus called Himself "the Light," and said that "the Light is the test by which men are guilty or not. People love darkness more than the Light because the things they do are sinful" (John 3:19 NLV). When you live differently than the world, people's consciences begin to bother them. And, in many cases, rather than changing their ways, they'll attack *you*.

Expect the world to hate you. And, in response, love your enemies just like Jesus taught. It won't be easy, but you will shine your light in a dark place. And some of those enemies might ultimately come to know Jesus too.

• •

*Lord, when the world hates me, give me
the strength to show them Your love.*

Prayer in Hard Times

"O Lord God of Israel, You are right and good.
For some of us have been left alive to return, as
it is this day. See, we are guilty before You. No
one can stand before You because of this."
EZRA 9:15 NLV

The Old Testament timeline is tricky because the books aren't placed in chronological order. The book of Ezra, in the middle of the Old Testament, actually describes events that happened late in Jewish history.

The man Ezra was a priest who served people who'd returned to Jerusalem after the exile in Babylon. They'd been taken captive as punishment for sin—and now Ezra was horrified to learn that many people were still sinning by marrying foreigners who didn't worship God.

Ezra went straight to prayer, admitting that God's laws were good and confessing the people's failure to obey. Then, in God's strength, Ezra confronted them.

The problems of our day won't be fixed without God's help—and God's help comes to us when we pray. As a Christian teen, you have a role to play in solving society's problems. And it starts with talking to God.

Father, please send Your Spirit in power to my
nation. Draw many people to Yourself.

Accept the Challenge

And it came to pass at that time, when. . .Samuel was
lying down to sleep, that the LORD called Samuel.
1 SAMUEL 3:2–4 SKJV

• •

Samuel was confused, maybe even frightened. That night, the child had heard a mysterious voice call his name three times. Each time, Eli—the priest who had become Samuel's guardian and mentor—had denied the voice was his. The third time, Eli had said something that must have sent a chill through Samuel's bones: the voice was coming from God.

When the voice came again, Samuel responded with the words Eli had given him: "Speak, for Your servant hears" (1 Samuel 3:10 SKJV).

Do you ever sense God calling you to some pursuit or task, and you feel confused and frightened? Don't ever think you're "too young" to serve. Some of the Bible's greatest men—including David, Josiah, and Timothy—started making a difference at a young age. You don't have to be a gray-headed theologian to hear and obey God's voice: you can accept His challenge today.

Are you listening like Samuel did?

• •

Lord, may I never miss Your voice when
You call my name. Open my ears to hear
whatever plans You have for me.

Don't Worry

"Look at the birds in the sky. They do not plant seeds.
They do not gather grain. They do not put grain into
a building to keep. Yet your Father in heaven feeds
them! Are you not more important than the birds?"
MATTHEW 6:26 NLV

Worry can consume us. When you're awaiting a doctor's report, the results of a tryout, or a response to a college application, your head can fill up with "what if" scenarios that rarely go your way. Unsettled thoughts keep us up at night and distract us from living well in the present.

Do you recall what Jesus said? "I tell you this: Do not worry about your life. Do not worry about what you are going to eat and drink. Do not worry about what you are going to wear. Is not life more important than food? Is not the body more important than clothes?" (Matthew 6:25 NLV). Then Jesus spoke the words of today's scripture, assuring us that God the Father knows our needs and will meet them.

When you get to worrying, stop and think of all the times God has already provided for you. Know that He'll provide for your future as well.

Lord, I thank You for Your care.
Please help me not to worry.

Praying for Your Future

*Zacharias saw an angel of the Lord standing
on the right side of the altar where the special
perfume was burning. When he saw the angel,
Zacharias was troubled and afraid.*
LUKE 1:11–12 NLV

Imagine yourself serving God at church, as Zacharias
was, and suddenly seeing an angel. Your first instinct
might be to fall down in shock or maybe run away.
Old Zacharias was "troubled and afraid," so you'd be
in good company.

But the angel was bringing good news: "Zacharias,
do not be afraid. Your prayer has been heard. Your wife
Elizabeth will give birth to a son. You are to name him
John. You will be glad and have much joy. Many people
will be happy because he is born" (Luke 1:13–14 NLV). The
angel was describing John the Baptist, the forerunner
of Jesus, the answer to Zacharias' prayers.

What have you been praying for regarding the
future? As you wait for God's answers, keep serving—
and don't be surprised when He shows up in some
surprising way. In fact, you should count on it!

Lord, give me eyes to see Your answers to my prayers.

Persecution

"For the day of the LORD is near on all the nations.
As you have done, it shall be done to you. Your
reward shall return on your own head."
OBADIAH 15 SKJV

∙∙∙

The Bible never sugarcoats anything. It records hard truths like "in the world you shall have tribulation" (John 16:33 SKJV) and "all who will live godly in Christ Jesus shall suffer persecution" (2 Timothy 3:12).

Classmates might snicker at you for following Jesus. You could lose a job for holding biblical beliefs. You might ultimately be imprisoned or killed for your faith. That's the bad news. The good news is twofold.

First, God is planning retribution for those who trouble His own. The nation of Edom learned that, painfully, when Obadiah's prophecy played out. Second, the worst-case scenario of persecution—your death—just ushers you into heaven. You'll be in the immediate presence of Jesus, with an eternity of perfection ahead.

Life in this world may be, and often is, hard. But God has you covered. One way or another, better days are coming.

∙∙∙

Lord God, give me the courage and grace to
honor You throughout times of persecution.

Moving Mountains

*Jesus said to them, "Have faith in God. For sure,
I tell you, a person may say to this mountain,
'Move from here into the sea.' And if he does
not doubt, but believes that what he says will be
done, it will happen. Because of this, I say to you,
whatever you ask for when you pray, have faith
that you will receive it. Then you will get it."*
MARK 11:22–24 NLV

• •

When life gets tough, it's easy to fall into a "woe is me" mindset. We might even begin to doubt that our faith is real.

Rest assured, though—God's grace is absolutely sufficient to overcome your doubts, your weaknesses, your apathy, and your outright disobedience. When it feels like the world around you is crumbling, call out to your Savior for protection. When the weight of guilt and shame press down on you, cry out to God for rest.

Faith is the key. Believe that God is, believe that He cares, believe that He has the resources to help you out. Ask without doubting, and see what mountains He moves.

• •

*Father, I know You want to help me through my
hardships. Today, I'm asking You to move mountains!*

Stand Against

Then Saul said to his servants, "Seek for
me a woman who is a medium, that I
may go to her and inquire of her."
1 SAMUEL 28:7 SKJV

• •

If you take the Bible seriously, you'll quickly run afoul
of the world's priorities. And not only in the realm of
sexual morality—there's also our culture's fascination
with the occult. What's up with all the witches and
wizards, astrology, and really dark, demonic stuff?

The answer is simple. People are moving further
and further away from God, cutting themselves off
from His love just as the disobedient King Saul did in
today's scripture. Without the Lord in their lives, they
turn to alternative sources of meaning and power.

This explains why God's Word is so strict about
witchcraft. Turning to some mystical power when life
gets hard is the ultimate way of saying, "God, I don't
need You anymore. I'm looking elsewhere."

But He is all we need—in this life or the next—no
matter what culture may say. Commit to God and His
Word, and you'll never go wrong.

• •

Lord, You are more than enough for me. Please help
me to stand against the pressure of the occult.

Need a Doctor?

*Jesus heard them and said, "People who
are well do not need a doctor."*
MATTHEW 9:12 NLV

We Christians can be hard on ourselves when we sin.
We fall short of our own image of perfection, and we
get frustrated. We begin to berate ourselves: *I can't
believe I did that!*

But note that, in today's scripture, Jesus said sinners are exactly the people He came to serve. Those
who believe they have everything together won't call
on Jesus. But He will gladly provide salvation to those
who know they are broken and stained by sin.

Don't forget: that's everybody. "For all men have
sinned and have missed the shining-greatness of God"
(Romans 3:23 NLV). You are not alone in your failures.

Jesus isn't shocked by your sin. But He doesn't
want to leave you in it, either. When you blow it, admit
it. Tell the Doctor that you're sick and need help. He'll
be there immediately with the cure.

*Heavenly Father, I know I am broken.
Thank You for sending Jesus to heal me
completely and make me a new person.*

Keep Awake!

*Watch and keep awake! Stand true to the
Lord. Keep on acting like men and be strong.
Everything you do should be done in love.*
1 CORINTHIANS 16:13–14 NLV

• •

No doubt you've heard about well-known Christians
who have fallen into sin. That can happen when we let
our guard down, allowing pride and physical desires to
get the best of us.

The apostle Paul didn't want that to happen to the
Christians in Corinth—or to anyone who would read his
letter in centuries to come. Paul wanted believers to
be proactive, to consciously stay on track spiritually.
So he called them to watch, to stay awake, to stand
true in the Lord.

We all have weaknesses, and Paul's command is
true for us too: Watch and keep awake! The devil is
on the prowl, looking for people to destroy. He'd
love nothing more than to lead *you* far from the Lord.
Don't let him!

• •

*Lord, I know my weaknesses. Give me
the strength to stay true to You.*

Rooted

That Christ may dwell in your hearts by faith, that you, being rooted and grounded in love, may be able to comprehend with all saints what is the breadth and length and depth and height, and to know the love of Christ, which surpasses knowledge, that you might be filled with all the fullness of God.
EPHESIANS 3:17–19 SKJV

• •

The roots of a tree provide stability and assist with nourishment. They draw up water and nutrients from the soil to help the tree grow. If the roots spread deep and wide, the tree becomes healthier and sturdier, able to stand against strong winds. A well-rooted tree provides benefits to its environment, offering shade and converting carbon dioxide into oxygen.

The apostle Paul used this idea of rootedness in his letter to the Ephesians. Christians, he said, should be "rooted and grounded" in God's love by their faith in Jesus Christ. We understand all of these things through God's Word, which nourishes us, helps us grow, and keeps us strong in the storms of life. And then we'll even provide benefit to our community, offering protection and the fresh air of faith.

• •

Lord, root me in Your truth. Help me to be diligent in studying Your Word.

Stretch, Don't Break

"For when I have brought them into the land
that flows with milk and honey. . .they will
turn to other gods and serve them."
DEUTERONOMY 31:20 SKJV

Humanity has a long history of abusing God's kindness. In troubled times, we long for health and prosperity—but when God blesses us, we often take it for granted and drift away from Him.

Is it any surprise that our lives sometimes get tough? After all, God is more concerned with our eternal well-being than any temporary satisfaction we seek (see 2 Corinthians 4:17).

The Christian faith is built on the truth that suffering has value. (Consider the Crucifixion.) Through the centuries, God's church has been like elastic rubber: the more the world tries to squash it, the wider it grows. But when left undisturbed, it tends to dry out and shrink, not living up to its true purpose.

Whenever life gets hard for you, thank God for putting on some pressure—He might be using that to draw you closer to Himself and make you more effective in this world.

Thank You, Father, for not allowing me to
stagnate in my faith. When the pressure's
on, may I stretch but not break.

Stay in Place

*Even when the cloud stayed over the meeting
tent for two days, or a month, or a year the
people of Israel would stay in that place and not
leave. They would leave when it was lifted.*

NUMBERS 9:22 NLV

• •

Youth is a time of energy and opportunity. It's hard to
sit still when there's so much life to be lived.

And yet. . .sometimes sitting still is exactly what
God wants of us.

The ancient Israelites, on their journey to the
"promised land" of Canaan, had to cool their heels
when God said "stop." His pillar of cloud and fire, which
rested above their worship tent called the tabernacle,
was the indicator. If it stayed put, the Israelites did too.
When it moved, they moved.

Waiting on the Lord is an important part of
Christian living. It shows our trust in Him, even when
we don't understand what He's doing. Waiting is difficult, to be sure. But you don't want to race ahead of
God and make trouble for yourself. The Lord loves you
and always wants what's best for you. So stay in place
until He tells you it's time to move.

• •

*Lord, please give me patience and a
spirit tuned to Your direction.*

Ask God

*That night God showed Himself to Solomon and said
to him, "Ask Me for anything and I will give it to you."*
2 CHRONICLES 1:7 NLV

• •

Is there some really heavy problem you've been battling? Do you ever feel worn out and in serious need of encouragement? God wants to help you.

The offer in today's scripture was made specifically to Solomon, as the young man followed his father, David, onto the throne of Israel. But the Bible makes plenty of other, similar offers of God's blessing to *you*.

Jesus, Emmanuel, "God with us," told His followers to ask, seek, and knock, expecting His Father's response (Matthew 7:7–8). Jesus also said that God cares and provides for all the birds of the earth—and that you are worth more than many birds (Luke 12:24).

Whatever it is that you need, take it to God in prayer. He's listening, and He's promised to help.

• •

*Father, please strengthen me for the heaviness
of life. Give me strength and patience as
You work out Your plan of provision.*

Watch What You Eat

"Test your servants for ten days. Give us only vegetables to eat and water to drink. Then compare how we look with the young men who are eating the king's best food."
DANIEL 1:12–13 NLV

This world will layer stress after stress on you. Don't add trouble by eating junk.

Everyone knows Daniel survived a night in the lions' den. Shadrach, Meshach, and Abednego went through a fiery furnace unharmed. But before those famous victories, the four young men had refused the fancy foods of Babylon. They were being trained for service in a nation that had overrun their homeland of Judah. They chose to honor God by saying "no" to foods He'd forbidden.

Daniel and company had only vegetables and water for ten days. They ultimately looked better than the guys who consumed Babylon's delicacies.

This story isn't a call to vegetarianism. But it does show that our eating is a way to honor God and help ourselves. Eat good foods in moderation. You'll be better equipped to face the challenges of your world.

Father, give me a taste for food that's truly good for me. I want to honor You in what I eat.

Your Circle of Friends

And they departed from there and passed through Galilee, and He did not want any man to know about it. For He was teaching His disciples.
MARK 9:30–31 SKJV

• •

Take a moment and think about your closest friends, people you really, truly, deeply trust. Maybe they're family members or classmates or guys at church, those you're comfortable sharing your highs and lows with. If Jesus were creating that list, He'd name Peter, James, and John, the "inner circle" of His twelve disciples.

There are times in life when things get really tough. These are the times you'll really benefit from the fellowship of your own inner circle. Jesus spent time with massive crowds, with numbers of guests at dinner parties and weddings, with His dozen disciples, and with "the three." Peter, James, and John were the ones with whom Jesus shared His most private moments.

The lesson for us? Be authentic with everyone, transparent to some, and intimate with only a few.

• •

Lord, please give me a few close friendships. Help me to sharpen those guys as they sharpen me.

Giving It to God

"Be of good courage, and let us behave valiantly for our people and for the cities of our God. And let the LORD do what is good in His sight."
1 CHRONICLES 19:13 SKJV

. . . .

King David sent servants carrying condolences to the king of Ammon, after the death of Hanun's father. Hanun foolishly took David's servants and "cut off their garments in the middle, at their buttocks, and sent them away" (1 Chronicles 19:4 SKJV). Then, assuming that David would be furious over this insult, the Ammonites prepared for war. David had no choice but to defend himself.

Have you ever been mistreated like that? Maybe you showed kindness toward someone, only for that person to publicly humiliate you. In such situations, how should you respond?

Joab, David's army commander, offered a valuable answer: "Be of good courage. . .and let the LORD do what is good in His sight." Joab did his assigned duties, but handed the battle over to God, trusting in His ultimate resolution. That's the best thing we can do too.

. . . .

Lord, if my enemies repay my kindness with mockery, help me check my anger and forgive them. I know that You have the final say.

The Heavy Lifting

*Then the Lord said to him, "Who has made man's
mouth? Who makes a man not able to speak or
hear? Who makes one blind or able to see? Is
it not I, the Lord? So go now. And I will be with
your mouth. I will teach you what to say."*
EXODUS 4:11–12 NLV

At certain times in our lives we'll face challenges that
we know will be tough to overcome. Then there are
the moments when we face impossible challenges we
know we can't rise above.

The Bible hero Moses felt like he couldn't accomplish what God had called him to do—lead the people
of Israel out of their slavery in Egypt. Moses tried to
wiggle out of the job, telling God he was unequipped
to handle the task. But God's response was simple.
He said, basically, *You don't have to do it. I will do it
through you.*

Our seemingly insurmountable challenges are
winnable. Just keep in mind that if God is calling you
to some task, He will do the heavy lifting to bring you
through.

*Thank You, Lord, that You have the wisdom
and strength to get me through any challenge.
I only need to let You work in me.*

Keep Growing

Growing strong in body is all right but growing in God-like living is more important. It will not only help you in this life now but in the next life also.
1 TIMOTHY 4:8 NLV

Young Timothy had great potential, but he needed to rise above some personal weaknesses. In fact, in the verse prior to today's scripture, Paul warned Timothy against believing "old wives' fables" (1 Timothy 4:7 SKJV). That's a phrase from way back, referring to silly urban legends that get passed on from one generation to the next. Paul urged Timothy to resist such untruths. Instead, he should begin the long, hard battle to grow as a Christian.

We live in a false world, where many will try to draw you away from the Lord. Are old wives' fables coming from your peers? Or worse, from misguided adults? Resist them all. "God-like living" is far more important, and you'll find everything you'll need for that in the Bible. Its truth will make you strong, and as you act on what you learn, you'll keep growing. That will "not only help you in this life now but in the next life also."

Lord, as I tune my ears to You and Your Word, I want to discover spiritual treasures that will last forever.

Stay Strong

We are proud of you and tell the other churches about you. We tell them how your faith stays so strong even when people make it hard for you and make you suffer.

2 Thessalonians 1:4 NLV

• •

You're just trying to be a "good Christian guy". . .and the world goes nuts. Everyone it seems—from politicians and entertainers to the kids at school—consider you as some kind of monster.

That's nothing new. During the apostle Paul's day, the Thessalonians were persecuted for following Jesus. Paul said he was proud of their faithfulness in spite of suffering. Though the battle was tough, God guaranteed they would ultimately win. "He does what is right and will allow trouble to come to those who are making it hard for you," Paul wrote. "He will help you and us who are suffering. . . . He will punish those who do not know God and those who do not obey the Good News of our Lord Jesus Christ" (2 Thessalonians 1:6–8 NLV).

In short: God is with you, He will protect you, and one day He will punish your enemies. Your faith in Him will bring you through the trials you face.

• •

Father, help me to stay strong in persecution.
May I never forget that You're always with me.

The Battlefield of Faith

You therefore endure hardship as a
good soldier of Jesus Christ.
2 TIMOTHY 2:3 SKJV

• •

August 16, 1940, in the skies over England. It's business as usual for Flight Lieutenant James Nicolson, patrolling near Southampton, eyes peeled for German aircraft.

Suddenly, four cannon shells tear through Nicolson's cockpit. He is cut to the bone, and his plane is burning. But as Nicolson prepares to bail out, he spots a German plane ahead.

Forgetting his escape, he gives chase, hoping to down the enemy before his own plane fails. Nicolson parachutes only when his skin begins to burn. He will ultimately recover from life-threatening injuries and receive the Victoria Cross from King George VI.

Warfare was different in the apostle Paul's day, but he had a similar kind of bravery in mind when he wrote to Timothy. Paul wanted the young man to fight intense battles for Christ in a culture that hated the gospel.

This world will spit the fire of doubt, temptation, and mockery. It's our duty to hang on. Know that your King is watching, eager to grant you an eternal award.

• •

Lord, help me stay in the fight against the
forces of darkness. I know Your reward
will make everything worth it.

No Good Deed
Goes Unpunished

*"For since I went to Pharaoh to speak in
Your name, he has hurt these people. You
have not set Your people free at all."*
EXODUS 5:23 NLV

• •

Ever hear somebody speak the title of today's devotional? Sometimes it does seem that obeying God and His expectations brings trouble into our lives.

That's how Moses felt when God told him to demand that Egypt's pharaoh release the Israelites from their slavery. Moses obeyed—and Pharaoh reacted by making the Israelites' work even harder. He told his overseers, "Do not give the people straw for making clay blocks any more. Let them go and gather straw for themselves" (Exodus 5:7 NLV).

That's probably not how Moses imagined the scenario playing out. But keep in mind that Moses did ultimately lead the Israelites out of Egypt.

When we try to serve God, things might not go well. But keep serving anyway. You never know what God's plan may be.

• •

*Father, empower me to keep serving You
regardless of the immediate outcome.*

It Is Written

Jesus said to the devil, "It is written, 'You must not tempt the Lord your God.'" When the devil finished tempting Jesus in every way, he went away from Jesus for awhile.
LUKE 4:12–13 NLV

• •

When Jesus was tempted for forty days in the desert, Satan tried everything. He tried to get the Lord to break his fast. Satan offered Jesus the entire world. When that didn't work, the devil urged Jesus to jump from the highest part of the temple, saying the angels would protect Him. Jesus quoted scripture to defeat each temptation. Eventually, Satan gave up and went away.

Are you being tempted right now? Are you using scripture to respond? God's Word has guidance for every aspect of life. If you aren't sure exactly what it says to your situation, use a concordance or an online search feature to find scriptures to throw back at Satan.

Save those verses—in your phone or the flyleaf of your Bible—where you can refer to them often. They are your best weapon against temptation.

• •

Lord, help me to know what You say about the temptations I face.

Don't Be Afraid of Their Faces

*"Do not be afraid of their faces, for I am
with you to rescue you," says the LORD.*
JEREMIAH 1:8 SKJV

• •

Guys don't like to admit they're afraid of anything.
But almost everyone, everywhere, finds something
frightening. And often that "something" is simply
other people's reactions to us.

When God called Jeremiah to be a prophet, the
young man—maybe only a teenager himself—claimed
he was just "a child" (Jeremiah 1:6). But God answered
with the interesting words of today's scripture. You
might think Jeremiah would be afraid of people's
balled-up fists or maybe their karate-kicking feet.
But the Lord specifically said, "Do not be afraid of
their *faces*." How could their sneers or snickering harm
Jeremiah? Especially when you consider that God was
with him.

The smile of God far outweighs the frown of
any human being. If people look at you funny, take
it straight to your heavenly Father. He is with you to
rescue you.

• •

*Lord God, I don't like it when people look at me funny.
But I also know that that can't hurt me. Give me the
courage to do right regardless of people's reaction.*

The Gift of Rest

The Lord is my Shepherd. I will have everything
I need. He lets me rest in fields of green grass.
He leads me beside the quiet waters.
PSALM 23:1–2 NLV

• •

Have you ever sat down next to a gentle creek or
river just to rest? There's something relaxing about
the sound of those rippling waters. In Psalm 23 we
see that rustling grass is just as peaceful. Truly, rest is
a gift from God, our Good Shepherd.

The life of a teenager can be hectic. Schoolwork,
sporting events, jobs, youth group trips, and family
functions can pull you in many directions, stretching
you mentally, physically, and emotionally. That's why
it's so important to allow God to lead us to moments
of rest.

In those quiet places, God can get our full attention. He can speak truth, love, and peace into our lives.
Why not set aside a specific time, at least once a week,
to truly just rest with Him?

• •

Lord, lead me to find rest this week. Help
me to quiet my mind, heart, soul, and
body so that You can work in me.

Prison Pal

Only Luke is with me.
2 TIMOTHY 4:11 SKJV

. . . .

The Bible doesn't say a whole lot about Luke, but this verse reveals much about his character.

The apostle Paul found himself in prison for his gospel-preaching efforts. He knew that execution was the likely end. Perhaps even worse, nearly everyone had abandoned Paul. . .everyone except Luke, that is. The "beloved physician" (Colossians 4:14) chose to stay, providing Paul company during what might have been his final days.

Whenever life gets hard—which is often—it's easy to forget that others are struggling too. Maybe there's a guy in your class who sits by himself and never talks to anyone. Maybe you have a friend who's facing a life-altering circumstance. Or maybe you just notice that a neighbor is looking sad lately.

If so, you don't need to offer profound advice or pretend you have all the answers. Just smile and ask how they're doing. A brief visit might change their day, week, or year for the better.

If you see a Paul in need, be a Luke.

. . . .

Lord, help me to provide encouragement to anyone who needs it, just as You encourage me.

Know Your God

Then the Lord passed by in front of [Moses],
saying, "The Lord, the Lord God, with loving-
pity and loving-favor, slow to anger, filled
with loving-kindness and truth."
EXODUS 34:6 NLV

Some days are just tough. Maybe you're feeling lonely. Maybe some sin is troubling your spirit. Maybe there's tension within your home. Whenever you're feeling down, it helps to know your God.

Take a moment to think about who God really is. What qualities come to mind? Do you see Him as a strict and distant father? Or maybe an all-powerful wish-fulfiller? Misconceptions won't help us, so let's see what God says about Himself.

When Moses met God on Mount Sinai, the Lord was so unfathomable that He offered up descriptive phrases to help Moses understand Him. God said He was gracious, compassionate, slow to anger, and full of love and faithfulness. All of those traits were shown in Jesus, God in human flesh, when He lived on earth— then died on the cross to pay the price for your sins.

Some days are tough. But with a God like this, you don't need to stress. He will see you through them.

Lord God, I am struggling. Please send
encouragement by Your Spirit. I trust You will.

Stay on Mission

But when Sanballat the Horonite, Tobiah the Ammonite servant, and Geshem the Arab heard about it, they made fun of us and hated us. They said, "What is this thing you are doing? Are you turning against the king?"
NEHEMIAH 2:19 NLV

. . . .

The story of Nehemiah shows that service to God often brings opposition. Don't be surprised if it happens to you too.

Nehemiah was a Jewish exile in Persia, the cupbearer to the king who got permission to travel to Jerusalem to rebuild the ravaged city's walls and gates. Before long, enemies arose to belittle Nehemiah's efforts and to try to frighten him into stopping the work.

But Nehemiah had an answer for them: "The God of heaven will make it go well for us. So we His servants will get up and build. But you have no share or right or anything to be remembered in Jerusalem" (Nehemiah 2:20 NLV).

Never lose focus on the mission God gives you. Even when others mock, God is still in control. He will remember you; anyone who refuses His grace will be completely forgotten.

. . . .

*Lord, when I face mockery for obeying
You, keep me on mission.*

No End in Sight

*Save me, O God, for the waters have come into my
soul. I sink in deep mire, where there is no standing.
I have come into deep waters, where the floods
overflow me. I am weary of my crying; my throat
is dried; my eyes fail while I wait for my God.*
PSALM 69:1–3 SKJV

· ·

When life gets tough, you might not see any end in
sight. Even a Bible hero like David felt that way. Here
in Psalm 69, his cry feels desperate, almost hopeless.
Perhaps you've known—or know—that feeling.

David, though, recognized the way through the
struggle was by honoring God. By the end of Psalm
69, he said, "I will praise the name of God with a song
and will magnify Him with thanksgiving. This also shall
please the LORD better than an ox or bull that has
horns and hooves. The humble shall see this and be
glad, and the heart of those who seek God shall live.
For the LORD hears the poor and does not despise His
prisoners" (verses 30–33 SKJV).

You can be honest with God about your sadness,
anger, and confusion. But never stop praising Him.

· ·

*God, when I feel hopeless, give me strength
and peace—because You are great!*

Misplaced Trust

*And Satan stood up against Israel and
provoked David to count Israel.*
1 CHRONICLES 21:1 SKJV

• •

The Bible doesn't say why God didn't want David to count the Israelites. While it could have been for some reason specific to the time and place, the more probable explanation is that God knew a census would boost David's ego and increase his confidence in his own army.

Just as God had whittled down Gideon's much larger force to three hundred soldiers, He may have been telling David, "Don't misplace your trust. *I've got this.*"

We all face times when we're tempted to put our trust in something other than God. Maybe your grades are tanking, a friendship is dissolving, or your family is experiencing turbulence. Satan loves to whisper in your ear, "God's abandoned you. Look elsewhere for help!"

That's a lie, of course. Even if it *seems* like God has packed up and left, He's always right beside you, urging you to keep trusting Him. Keep your faith where it belongs—in God Himself—and the battle is already won.

• •

*Thank You, Lord, for fighting my battles.
Help me to rely on You and You alone.*

Run!

The lips of a strange woman are as sweet as
honey. Her talk is as smooth as oil. But in the
end she is as bitter tasting as wormwood, and
as sharp as a sword that cuts both ways.
PROVERBS 5:3–4 NLV

• •

Far too many a Christian man has lost his wife, family, and reputation after giving in to a sexual relationship outside his marriage. These men didn't do what King Solomon advised in Proverbs 5:8 (NLV): "Keep far away from her. Do not go near the door of her house."

Right now, you're only a teenager—marriage may seem far in the future. But now is the time to develop habits that will protect yourself and the wife God may give you. Think of young Joseph in Egypt, who ran out of the house when Potiphar's wife tried to seduce him (Genesis 39:12). You can run—literally or figuratively—from sexual temptations, whether they come from your own thoughts, a girl you know, or pornography.

Today's scripture describes immorality as seemingly sweet, but ultimately bitter. Take steps now to protect yourself later.

• •

Lord, help me to honor and please
You with my body. May I run from any
situation that might cause me to sin.

You're Being Watched

"For the eyes of the Lord move over all the earth so that He may give strength to those whose whole heart is given to Him."
2 CHRONICLES 16:9 NLV

It's been said that "character is who you are when no one is watching." But in reality, you're *always* being watched—by the all-seeing, all-knowing God of the universe.

For some people, that's a frightening idea. But for committed followers of Jesus, it's a beautiful thing. God is constantly scanning the whole earth, looking for "people whose whole heart is given to Him." Why? So that "He may give strength" to them.

This world is no friend of God or of anyone who wants to live for Him. But God is far bigger, far better, far worthier than anything in this dark, depressing, broken world—and He has promised to fill you up when everything else drains you dry.

Show your good character by doing good when nobody else sees. But know that God is watching, and He's preparing your reward.

Father, I thank You for seeing me. I ask for the strength You promise to help me succeed.

A World Out of Whack

*The vine dries up and the fig tree wastes away. The
pomegranate, the palm, the apple tree, and all the
trees of the field dry up. And the people's joy dries up.*
JOEL 1:12 NLV

• •

Tough times in our personal lives are hard enough. But
often the whole world seems out of whack. When the
national economy is teetering or terrorists are snarling
threats or wars are flaring up around the world, "people's joy dries up" in the words of Joel.

Nobody likes hard times, but as a Christian, you can
trust they have a purpose. In Joel's time, the drought
and famine and weeping were intended to bring sinful
people back to God. Your own hardships may have the
same purpose. Or maybe God is just building your
trust-muscles. No matter what, you can be sure that
"God makes all things work together for the good of
those who love Him and are chosen to be a part of His
plan" (Romans 8:28 NLV).

• •

*Heavenly Father, my eyes see all kinds of bad
in the world. Please open my heart to the good
You're doing in and through every circumstance.*

Feeling Forsaken?

*My God, my God, why have You forsaken
me? Why are You so far from helping me
and from the words of my groaning?*
PSALM 22:1 SKJV

Some of Jesus' final words on the cross were, "My
God, my God, why have You forsaken Me?" (Matthew
28:46 SKJV). That's a very real, heart-wrenching cry
from Jesus to His Father.

Has there ever been a time when *you* cried out to
God, "Why have You forsaken me? Why have You left
me alone?" If so, you're clearly in very good company.
Jesus' painful cry was a quote from Israel's great king
and psalm writer, David.

Many of us will feel forsaken by God at some time
or another: life is going crazy and God seems silent.
We feel like we're entirely on our own.

But that's not true. God *never* abandons those who
follow Jesus. Strange as it may seem, God the Father
did turn His back on His Son, as Jesus bore the sins of
the whole world. But with Jesus' willing sacrifice made,
the sin debt paid, there's no need for God to forsake
you if you are in Christ. Even when you feel alone,
you're not—and God will make that plain soon enough.

Lord God, thank You for never leaving me!

Undeserved Blessing

And David. . .said, "Who am I, O LORD God, and what
is my house, that You have brought me this far?"
1 CHRONICLES 17:16 SKJV

• •

Ever had a time when you were amazed at how all the
pieces fell in place to resolve a difficult situation? If
not, can you imagine how nice that would be? Then
you can understand what David felt whenever he spoke
the words of today's scripture.

David's life was thornier than most of ours put
together. Not only was he a king with heavy responsibilities, there were a host of enemies who wanted
his head on a platter. And he didn't help himself with
some of his personal decisions (*see* Bathsheba).

But in spite of all this, God promised David that his
kingdom would endure—that He would bring an eternal
king (Jesus) from David's line. What could David do
other than praise God for such mercy?

His response sets the standard for us today. When
God delivers us from a trial, when He forgives our
blunders, when He shows us undeserved blessing,
our first instinct should be to humble ourselves and
to lift Him up.

• •

Lord, I thank You for all the blessings I don't deserve.
Help me never to lose sight of Your goodness.

Be a Peacemaker

A soft answer turns away wrath,
but harsh words stir up anger.
PROVERBS 15:1 SKJV

• •

We've all had arguments with friends or family members. There's a split second in which we can decide to raise the level of the argument or cool it down. As a Spirit-led Christian, you can always choose a gentle answer: "The fruit of the Spirit is love, joy, peace, long-suffering, gentleness, goodness, faith, meekness, self-control" (Galatians 5:22–23 SKJV).

We as Christians can and should be peacemakers. Think how your unbelieving friends might be influenced when they see you stop potential fights with a gentle answer. The tongue has far more power than most people realize, as today's scripture indicates. By what you say, you can turn anger aside or make a bad situation worse.

Choose wisely.

• •

Lord, Your Spirit lives inside me—please help me
to show people what that means. I want to be
loving and gentle in tense situations, kind to
others even if they're not. May I be a peacemaker
for other people's benefit and for Your glory.

Because God Is Good

It was not because we worked to be right with God. It was because of His loving-kindness that He washed our sins away. At the same time He gave us new life when the Holy Spirit came into our lives.
Titus 3:5 NLV

• •

If, out of the blue, a friend gave you a really cool gift, how would you respond? Hopefully, you'd say "thank you." But would you then start thinking, *Oh, man—I need to find a gift to give in return*. . . . At that point, the concept of "a gift" has morphed into "a trade."

Lots of people do that with friends and relatives. Lots of people try to do that with God.

We try to "earn" our salvation by our good works. Or we might punish ourselves when we do wrong. But God's gift of salvation is and always was free—as is His gift of forgiveness for the sins we still commit (see 1 John 1:9).

Never forget: God doesn't love us because we're good or make up for our wrongs. He loves us because *He* is good. And Jesus has already paid the price for our every sin.

• •

Heavenly Father, remind me that Jesus died for all I have ever done. Thank You for the new life You provide through Him.

What He's Done

"For the life of the flesh is in the blood. I have given it to you on the altar to make your souls free from sin. For the blood makes you free from sin because of the life in it."
LEVITICUS 17:11 NLV

. . . .

You may have heard someone say (or thought it yourself), "Leviticus is just a book of rules." There's some truth to that statement, but Leviticus is also a book of love. You see, before Jesus died on the cross, the only way to receive forgiveness was to present a blood sacrifice to God. His rule was an innocent animal life for a guilty human life. Then, when the time was right, God sent His Son to *be* the once-for-all blood sacrifice that would provide grace, forgiveness, and mercy forever.

What He's done is the greatest act of forgiveness in the history of the world. Let's show our gratitude by surrendering our minds and bodies and plans, every day, as a sacrifice to Him.

. . . .

Father, I thank You for providing Jesus as the ultimate sacrifice. Without Him, my life is hopeless. With Him in my life, I have purpose and meaning for all eternity.

Stay Away from the Edge

But every man is tempted when he is drawn
away by his own lust and enticed. . . . And sin,
when it is finished, brings forth death.
JAMES 1:14–15 SKJV

. . . .

Soaring 876 feet above the river below, West Virginia's New River Gorge Bridge is one of the highest on the planet. It has become a popular tourist destination, with numerous trails nearby. Some of these trails wind along the edges of absurdly high cliffs, providing breathtaking glimpses of the terrain.

These breathtaking sights, though, can produce breathtaking danger. For inexperienced hikers, the cliff's edge may become a challenge for which they are not prepared. Since the heights involved are so vast, one small slip can prove fatal.

Today's scripture warns against the alluring draw of sin. Like a cliff's edge, sin tempts you to get as close as possible without falling.

But no matter how enticing the call, don't give in. Don't ponder how close you can get to the edge without tumbling over. Instead, let God be your guide. If He says to stay away, stay away—then don't wander back.

. . . .

Father, I don't want to even entertain the idea
of sinning. Give me the power to resist.

For Richer or Poorer

The rich and the poor meet together.
The Lord is the maker of them all.
PROVERBS 22:2 NLV

. . . .

Maybe you come from a well-to-do family. You have plenty of money for your needs and for your wants. If so, thank God for that blessing.

Many more people struggle with the family budget. Your house needs repairs, your car is older, you feel like your clothes are getting faded and out of date. You might even struggle to buy groceries.

Here's what an old-time Bible commentator, Matthew Henry, had to say about money: the Lord Himself will "make some poor, to exercise their patience, and contentment, and dependence upon God, and others rich, to exercise their thankfulness and beneficence"—their generosity and willingness to do good.

Both wealth and poverty bring challenges to us as Christians. Wherever you fall on the money spectrum, make sure you keep your focus on God. Rich or poor, "the Lord is maker of them all."

. . . .

Lord, I don't ever want money—too much
or too little—to pull me away from You.
Please keep me close to Your heart.

Punished for. . .Doing Right?

*This shows you have received loving-favor
when you are even punished for doing what
is right because of your trust in God.*
1 PETER 2:19 NLV

• •

You've probably heard about a committed Christian who lost his job or found legal problems for standing by his biblical principles. Maybe *you've* taken heat for being a Christian. What's up with that?

Nobody wants to suffer for doing right, but we can't say we were never warned. Peter was talking about that almost two thousand years ago.

Some early Christians were "punished for doing right because of [their] trust in God." But notice the first part of today's verse: "This shows you have received loving-favor"—from God. Peter went on to say that "if you are beaten when you have done what is right, and do not try to get out of it, God is pleased" (1 Peter 2:20 NLV).

Why? Because then you're following in Jesus' footsteps: "When people spoke against Him, He never spoke back. When He suffered from what people did to Him, He did not try to pay them back. He left it in the hands of the One Who is always right in judging" (1 Peter 2:23 NLV).

• •

*Father, may I always reflect You and trust
in Your promise to bring justice.*

When Losses Come

*In the year that King Uzziah died I also saw
the Lord sitting on a throne, high and lifted
up, and His train filled the temple.*

Isaiah 6:1 skjv

• •

Losses are tough enough in unimportant things like
sports. But when losses hit close to home—when someone important to us dies or fails morally—they can be
devastating.

Isaiah probably felt a double loss when King Uzziah
passed away. The longest serving ruler of Judah, Uzziah
had done much good. But in the end, pride derailed
him. Uzziah died a leper after offering incense in the
temple, a job reserved for the priests. His moral failure
and death were undoubtedly troubling to a faithful
citizen like Isaiah.

But notice what God did. He gave an incredible
vision of Himself to Isaiah. The old-time Bible teacher
Matthew Henry wrote that "Israel's king dies, but
Israel's God still lives. . . . King Uzziah dies in a hospital,
but the King of kings still sits upon His throne."

Whatever losses come your way, know that your
King is still in control.

• •

*Lord God, You are all-powerful and eternal. Thank You
for being over and above everything that I experience.*

Work for It

*Work for the things that make peace and help
each other become stronger Christians.*
ROMANS 14:19 NLV

. . . .

If you get tired, frustrated, and angry with the world,
you can be sure others do too. That's why it's so
important for Christians to pull together for help and
encouragement.

Has a friend been mocked for his faith? Stand up
for him! You'd want someone to stand up for you. Is a
fellow believer going down a wrong path in terms of his
attitude, behavior, or theology? Reach out, with love
and compassion, to try to get him back on track. And
if someone approaches *you* with similar concerns, be
sure you consider what they have to say. These are all
important elements of Christian fellowship.

Don't expect this to be easy. Notice that the first
word of today's verse is *work*. But you know that all
good things take time and effort. When you do the
hard things God calls you to do, you're in line for His
blessing.

. . . .

*Lord, please help me to speak life, love, and grace
into every situation. I want to point people to You!*

Dealing with Guilt

And the LORD God said to the woman, "What is this that you have done?" And the woman said, "The serpent deceived me, and I ate."
GENESIS 3:13 SKJV

• •

"The devil made me do it."

The phrase gets thrown around casually, like a guy flippantly excuses a night of drunkenness. But it's even been used as a defense in court, as when Arne Cheyenne Johnson tried to excuse the murder of his landlord in 1981. However it's used, the speaker is trying to shift blame to someone else.

Have you ever been caught doing something you're not proud of? We all have—and it makes us miserable. Of course, it's best to simply avoid shame-making behaviors in the first place. But let's be honest—none of us does that perfectly. So instead of leveling blame at others, let's deal properly with our guilt—by confessing, repenting, and asking God for forgiveness.

That's when we can really put the past behind us and move on.

• •

God, please use my feelings of guilt to pull me closer to You. You're the only one who can clear me of my sin.

Your True Home

These people all died having faith in God. They did not receive what God had promised to them. But they could see far ahead to all the things God promised and they were glad for them. They knew they were strangers here. This earth was not their home.
HEBREWS 11:13 NLV

• •

Take a moment to read Hebrews 11:1–12, the verses immediately before today's scripture. They describe people like Abel, Enoch, Noah, Abraham, and Sarah, who all died without seeing every promise of God fulfilled. The entering of the promised land, the coming of the Messiah, and all the spiritual blessings we enjoy through Jesus were just hazy potentialities to these Old Testament heroes. They weren't perfect people, but they knew God was faithful—and they believed He would follow through on what He'd said. They viewed themselves simply as strangers on earth, knowing heaven was their true home.

It's easy to get caught up in the drama and trauma of this life. But God has made many promises that will be fulfilled in eternity. This life is not all there is. One day, you will be in the presence of Jesus, and you'll feel right at home.

• •

*Lord, I trust You to fulfill all Your promises. . .
even if I don't live long enough to see it.*

Don't Blend In

*Dear friend, do not follow what is sinful, but
follow what is good. The person who does
what is good belongs to God. The person who
does what is sinful has not seen God.*

3 John 11 nlv

• •

This world is a difficult place to be a follower of Jesus.
We want to be popular and liked—but what happens
when others push you to do things you know run
counter to Christianity? What if they think your faith
is lame or even something harmful?

Never forget that Jesus Himself—the only perfect human being in history—was mocked, hated, and
ultimately murdered. Maybe that sounds like a bad
advertisement for Christianity. . .but God promises an
eternal reward for anyone who follows Jesus faithfully,
through good and bad.

The apostle John calls believers to "follow what
is good," to be a shining light for Christ in this world.
Don't blend in, stand out. Others may ultimately want
to know what makes you different.

• •

*Lord, help me to be a good friend to those
who don't know You. May Your light shine
through me and draw them to salvation.*

The Cause of My Suffering

Do not leave me alone, O Lord! O my God, do not be far from me! Hurry to help me, O Lord, Who saves me!
PSALM 38:21–22 NLV

• •

Do you know where suffering comes from? Trials come in all shapes and sizes, but *why* do they happen?

Ultimately, suffering is caused by sin. Sometimes our own sin creates suffering. Every time, sin in general is behind the difficulties we face in this world.

You weren't created to experience suffering. But when Adam and Eve sinned in the garden of Eden, they opened the door to every hardship that you experience.

So what can we do? Remember that God never promised us ease and pleasure (John 16:33). But, through Jesus, we have been forgiven of our own sins (Matthew 26:28). We've been given the Holy Spirit to strengthen and encourage us (Acts 2:38). And we have total access to God the Father through prayer (Hebrews 4:16).

David, who wrote today's scripture, experienced plenty of suffering, some self-inflicted and much otherwise. But he knew where to turn for help, and it's the same place we should: the Lord who saves us.

• •

Father God, please help me through my struggles and empower me to live for You.

Choices, Choices

*"I call heaven and earth to witness this day against
you, that I have set before you life and death,
blessing and cursing. Therefore choose life, that
both you and your descendants may live."*
DEUTERONOMY 30:19 SKJV

A poll found that the average person spends about fifty minutes a week just trying to decide which television show or movie to watch. Don't think that sounds like a lot? Well, what happens when you extend one week out to a month? A year? A lifetime? If you do the math, you learn that many of us spend a total of *a hundred days* just browsing through entertainment options!

God knows how indecisive human beings are, so He whittled the most important options down to just two: life or death. Serve Him and live forever, or rebel and miss out on His presence. The choice should be the easiest decision in history, yet many people spend their entire lives trying to make up their minds.

When life is hard and your options seem unclear, don't waste your precious time fiddling with the spiritual remote—choose God, quickly and decisively. You'll enjoy His benefits forever.

*God, thank You for making the choice
to serve You an easy one.*

False Teachers

Turn away from foolish talk. Do not argue with those who think they know so much. They know less than they think they do. Some people have gone after much learning. It has proved to be false and they have turned away from the faith.
1 TIMOTHY 6:20–21 NLV

•••

The message of the Bible is pretty simple: God created people, people sinned, God made a way for people to return to Him through faith in Jesus Christ. But that simple message is delivered in a very large book that does include some confusing stuff.

Christian denominations have differing views on topics like the end times or the way to baptize. But if they hold to the basics of the faith, Christians of different stripes can view each other as family, getting along despite differences.

False teachers, though, deny important truths about God and Jesus. They twist the words of scripture to make things that are clear seem fuzzy. And there's a lot of that going on today.

The apostle Paul said you should simply walk away from those arguments. If someone is saying things that clearly aren't true—or even feel amiss—just leave the conversation. Dig into your Bible and pray for God's wisdom.

•••

Lord, give me discernment to recognize false teaching that would lead me far from You.

Rest in Jesus

"Come to Me, all of you who work and have heavy loads. I will give you rest. Follow My teachings and learn from Me. I am gentle and do not have pride. You will have rest for your souls."
MATTHEW 11:28–29 NLV

Do you feel it? The heavy load of schoolwork, a part-time job, school events, band or sports practice, activities with friends, family obligations. . .you name it. Teenagers are busy! It's easy to feel exhausted when there's so much going on in life.

The Jews of Jesus' day knew how that felt. Theirs was an occupied nation, and the people were not free to do as they chose. They were heavily taxed. They were expected to carry supplies for Roman soldiers when commanded. And their own religious leaders had so many rules it was hard to know if they were "okay with God."

But Jesus called them—as He calls us—to connect with Him. Take all of the stress and strain and give it to Jesus. That's how you find rest from the "heavy loads" of life.

Lord Jesus, sometimes I don't know how to slow down. Please help me to find rest in You.

Stay Faithful

*"The Lord God is my strength, and He will
make my feet like deer's feet, and He will
make me walk on my high places."*
HABAKKUK 3:19 SKJV

• •

Today's scripture is the high point of Habakkuk's prophecy. Don't you love the imagery of God strengthening you to scale mountains like a surefooted deer?

But this positive picture follows a whole lot of negativity. God condemned His people for violence, drunkenness, and idolatry, threatening them with punishment. Habakkuk couldn't argue with God's assessment, so he simply promised to stay faithful. "Although the fig tree shall not blossom, fruit shall not be on the vines, the labor of the olive shall fail, the fields shall yield no food, the flock shall be cut off from the fold, and there shall be no herd in the stalls, yet I will rejoice in the Lord. I will rejoice in the God of my salvation" (Habakkuk 3:17–18 SKJV).

Let's choose to be like Habakkuk. Whatever hardships we face, may we stay faithful and "rejoice in the Lord." Make the conscious choice to honor God first. *Then* you'll climb the mountains.

• •

*Father, help me choose to praise
and honor You in all I do.*

"I Belong to Christ"

*You were under the power of the Law. But now you
are dead to it because you are joined to another.
You are joined to Christ Who was raised from
the dead. This is so we may be what God wants
us to be. Our lives are to give fruit for Him.*
ROMANS 7:4 NLV

• •

The teen years are some of the most challenging in life.
Your identity is rapidly shapeshifting. Your confidence
level will be high one day and at rock bottom the next.
It can drive you half crazy.

But the more you understand your identity in
Christ, the more quickly these issues resolve. Jesus
wants to bless you through all the upheavals and challenges of life. When your focus is on Him, you can be
what God wants you to be.

The problem is that we often get distracted. When
our identity is found in things other than Jesus, life is
rocky at best. The difficulties and drama we encounter
fill our minds rather than who we are in Jesus. But the
apostle Paul says we were "joined" to Christ, who was
raised from the dead. What could be better and more
powerful than He is? Remind yourself that you belong
to Jesus, and your life will be fruitful.

• •

Jesus, help me to find my identity in You!

No Regrets

Remember now your Creator in the days of your youth.
ECCLESIASTES 12:1 SKJV

● ●

A poignant article from *Business Insider* highlights a series of interviews with elderly people discussing their biggest regrets. When the author asked, "Do you wish you had accomplished more?" one man answered, "No, I wish I loved more."

But I'm just a teenager, you might be thinking. *What does this have to do with me?* It's true that old age may seem like another world to you now—another universe, even. But just as the smallest mountain stream eventually arrives at the ocean, so you will one day wash up on the edge of eternity, wondering where your life has gone.

The chaos of today—its passions, arguments, frustrations, boredoms, relationships, breakups, and general craziness—will fade. But your responses will not. With every choice you make, a small part of your identity is either strengthened or diminished.

So today, "in the days of your youth," remember your Creator. Reflect His love back to Him and the people around you. You won't regret it.

● ●

Lord, I don't want to waste my life. Help me strive to please You in everything I do.

When You're Ticked Off

*He who is slow to anger is better than
the powerful. And he who rules his spirit
is better than he who takes a city.*
PROVERBS 16:32 NLV

• •

Think about a time when someone really ticked you off. Did you show any self-control? Could the other person see Jesus in your response? Or was there little difference between your reaction and an unbeliever's?

Anger isn't necessarily a sin. Jesus Himself overturned merchants' tables and chased them out of the temple for their greedy and disrespectful behavior. But, generally speaking, it's better to be slow to anger, even when someone has personally wronged us. A measured response shows that you are under the Holy Spirit's control. Even unbelievers notice that.

Commit now, before God, to think before you speak in anger. Ask for His help to display grace, peace, and forgiveness. You won't need to apologize later. . . and you might point someone toward salvation.

• •

*Lord, help me to control my tongue when people anger
me. I want the world to see You in my reactions.*

What Comes Next?

"Do not worry. Do not keep saying, 'What will we eat?' or, 'What will we drink?' or, 'What will we wear?' The people who do not know God are looking for all these things. Your Father in heaven knows you need all these things."
MATTHEW 6:31–32 NLV

The middle school and high school years can be tough. Things are constantly changing! Once you get a routine ironed out, it seems it all changes the next year. Then graduation appears on the horizon along with the stress of "what comes next." A teen guy's future is filled with life-changing transitions and all the uncertainty they bring.

Wherever you stand in the process, you're probably feeling a mixture of excitement and anxiety. Just remember this: no matter how you're feeling at the moment, God knows all about your future. Nothing that's coming for *you* is a surprise to *Him*.

Jesus has said that His followers don't need to worry about tomorrow, about whatever comes next. Focus on God's Kingdom, and He'll take care of all the details for you.

Lord, please prepare me to handle the transitions of the teen years. Help me to live for You as my life continues to unfold.

Help Your Friends

Have loving-kindness for those who doubt.
Save some by pulling them out of the fire.
JUDE 22–23 NLV

. . . .

Yes, life can be challenging. And not just to you alone.

It's safe to say that many of your friends are probably struggling right now. So what can you do when life gets tough for the people around you? When others are struggling with sin or to hold on to their faith?

Jude, who may have been a half brother of Jesus, urged you to "have loving-kindness for those who doubt" and "save some." To do that, get involved in their lives. Talk to them in love. But be sure to talk to God first in prayer.

The goal is to help your friends through the tough times. Direct their thoughts and focus back to Jesus. Always be sympathetic to their struggle, but never agree with any wrongdoing. As Jude says later in verse 23, "Be afraid of being led into doing their sins."

. . . .

Lord, please help me to see when others need
encouragement, and give me the ability to guide
them through tough times. Keep me strong so I
don't fall into their sin or doubt with them.

Don't Argue

But avoid foolish and ignorant questions,
knowing that they breed strife.
2 TIMOTHY 2:23 SKJV

• •

In 2015, an earthquake shook the internet, launching a heated debate that pitted friend against friend, family member against family member. What could possibly cause such upheaval? The answer may surprise you.

When the picture of a striped dress began circulating online, different people saw different colors. Some perceived blue and black while others thought it was white and gold. It was some kind of optical illusion, and scientists are still researching the phenomenon.

How often are Christians divided like that? Sometimes, it seems as if we care more about silly, unknowable things than we do about matters pertaining to salvation. Too often, the real issue takes a backseat to making sure everyone understands that "*my* answer should be believed." When pride enters our theology, ugly conflicts result.

Let's not make life any harder than it already is. As Christians, we have God's instruction (and help) to "live peaceably with all men" (Romans 12:18 SKJV). Make sure the things you feel most passionate about are truly *biblical* issues.

• •

Lord, it's okay if people don't always agree with me.
Help me learn to keep loving them just as You love me.

Coping with Trouble

Jehoshaphat was afraid and decided to call on the Lord. He made a special time of not eating in all Judah. And Judah gathered together to pray for help from the Lord. They came to the Lord from all the cities of Judah to call on the Lord.
2 CHRONICLES 20:3–4 NLV

What do you do in times of stress? Everyone has coping mechanisms. Some are almost automatic, deeply ingrained habits of fight or flight whenever we face a major challenge.

When Jehoshaphat, king of Judah, heard that the armies of three nations were coming to attack Jerusalem, he was understandably fearful. Jehoshaphat could have run away and hidden, or he could have eaten and drunk himself into an oblivious stupor. But instead he resolved to call on God. The king proclaimed a fast for all his people, urging them to stop eating to focus on praise and prayer. In the end, the Lord stepped in to rout the enemies of Israel.

Whenever you face a stressful situation, respond like Jehoshaphat. Turn to God in praise and prayer, and watch for the victory He'll send.

Lord God, I can't always see past my stressful situations. Please give me peace in the trial, and lead me to ultimate victory.

Fellowship

Let us help each other to love others and to do good.
Let us not stay away from church meetings. Some
people are doing this all the time. Comfort each
other as you see the day of His return coming near.
HEBREWS 10:24–25 NLV

• •

It's easy to play video games rather than get out and care for real, live people. It may seem better to sleep in on Sunday rather than attend church. It's more comfortable to try to overcome a sin on your own rather than seek help. But don't be fooled: Christians need each other.

Pastor and author John Piper says, "Fellowship is a mutual bond that Christians have with Christ that puts us in a deep, eternal relationship with one another." Since we belong to Christ, we also belong to other believers—eternally. We are supposed to help each other do good works. We are supposed to worship together and comfort one another as the day of Jesus' return gets closer.

You aren't meant to "do you." You are designed to be in fellowship with other Christians, so you can all spur each other onward. Get plugged in and experience the difference.

• •

Lord, when I'm tempted to pull away
from other believers, to do things on my
own, remind me of Your plan for us.

God Is Faithful

Then the LORD said to me, "Go again, love a woman who is beloved by her friend, yet an adulteress, just like the love of the LORD toward the children of Israel."

HOSEA 3:1 SKJV

. . . .

Some of our toughest challenges don't come from the world. They arise within us.

We are tempted to do wrong. We often fail. And then we struggle with the fact that—through Jesus Christ—we are accepted by God. If you have a hard time believing that, read through the story of Hosea. Go ahead—this can wait. . . .

Back again? God told His prophet Hosea to marry an adulteress, a woman who would cheat on him. And then God had Hosea track her down, buy her back from a slave market, and love her again. It was all a picture of God's love for His own people, the often foolish, cranky, and sinful Israelites.

If God was that committed to them, don't you think He'll be faithful to those of us who have chosen to follow His Son? Believe it—when you are in Jesus Christ, you're golden.

. . . .

Lord, I thank You for Your faithful love!

Your Safe Haven

*God is our safe place and our strength. He is
always our help when we are in trouble.*
PSALM 46:1 NLV

. . . .

When firefighters arrive at a burning building, the
incident commander quickly establishes a "safe haven"
for them. Often times located near an ambulance, this
is a spot to flee to if someone gets hurt or the fire
blazes out of control.

When your life gets dicey, what is your safe haven?
Maybe you retreat to your bedroom or perhaps there's
a quiet spot in the woods. Maybe you connect with a
particular friend or you call on your parents or youth
pastor.

All of these options have their benefits. But don't
forget the ultimate "safe place": God Himself. Run to
your favorite people and places when you need help,
but remember that, ultimately, God is "always our help
when we are in trouble."

Get alone with Him to read His Word and pray.
Give Him time to respond to your spirit. He'll provide
the strength and safety you need to overcome trouble.

. . . .

*Lord, You are my safe place and my strength.
Please help me to get through my trials.*

Invisible God

"Therefore be very careful yourselves, for you saw no kind of form on the day that the LORD spoke to you in Horeb out of the midst of the fire, lest you corrupt yourselves and make for yourselves an engraved image."
DEUTERONOMY 4:15–16 SKJV

Created in God's image, we all have an instinct to worship. Sadly, because of our fallen nature, many people overlook God altogether, choosing instead to fill the void with lesser things—"gods" of our own imagination.

The ancient Egyptians based their theology on bizarre, mythological creatures that supposedly intervened in human affairs. Today, in our more "enlightened" culture, our gods take the shape of celebrities, technology, political movements, and a thousand other things people look to for meaning.

Nothing has really changed.

When life gets hard, will you turn to some manmade god that can't hear or help you? Or will you look to the invisible yet absolutely real and powerful God who made you, loves you, and provides all you need?

Is that even a question?

Father, help me keep my spiritual eyes on You, even when my physical eyes can't detect Your presence.

You're in a War

Keep awake! Watch at all times. The devil is working against you. He is walking around like a hungry lion with his mouth open. He is looking for someone to eat.
1 PETER 5:8 NLV

• •

Do you ever wonder why life can be so hard? In the big picture, we know that sin is real and has warped our world. But why does trouble seem to find us in particular? The answer is simple: Satan and his demons have actively targeted you, like hungry lions on the prowl.

In his letter to the Ephesians, the apostle Paul noted that "our fight is not with people. It is against the leaders and the powers and the spirits of darkness in this world. It is against the demon world that works in the heavens" (Ephesians 6:12 NLV). Paul urged Christians to wear the "armor of God" for protection (see Ephesians 6:13–17).

If you feel as if there are powerful forces against you, there are. Life is not a stroll through the park when there are hungry lions after you. You're in a war!

• •

Heavenly Father, give me Your strength to help me stand strong in the battle. I want to win!

Take the Land

*Then Caleb told the people. . . "Let us
go up at once and take the land. For we
are well able to take it in battle."*

God had promised to give the land of Canaan to His people, the Israelites. But first, He told Moses to send twelve men—one leader from each tribe—to spy on the land. When they came back forty days later, they told Moses and the people that Canaan was indeed flowing with milk and honey, just as God had said. But, ten of the spies added, the cities had large walls around them, and there were giants living there. These spies weren't convinced that God's people were strong enough to take the land.

That's when Caleb showed what true leadership is. He stepped forward to say the ten spies were wrong. Caleb knew that when God has spoken, He will be faithful to His word. It didn't matter how strong Canaan's cities were or how big its people. None of them could stand against God's promises.

Nothing can stand against God's promises today, either. You can confidently pursue whatever He's offered you. Go ahead—take the land!

*Lord, give me the faith of Caleb to face
my own giants. With You, I can't lose.*

A New Hope

*I am sure that our suffering now cannot be compared
to the shining-greatness that He is going to give us.*
ROMANS 8:18 NLV

• •

Star Wars fans recognize the title of this devotional
as the subtitle of Episode IV, the first movie in the
long-running sci-fi franchise. (If you're wondering
why "episode four" is the *first* movie, you'll have to
do some research on your own. We don't have space
to explain here!)

The fictional galaxy, far, far away, needed hope to
deal with the evil empire headed by the likes of Darth
Vader. In our real galaxy, here and now, we need hope
as well. . .a hope that our faith in God provides.

The apostle Paul understood suffering—he wrote
several biblical books from a prison cell. He experienced arrests, beatings, stoning, and shipwreck through
the course of his ministry and somehow managed to
press on. How? He knew that God had something
much greater planned for him—and for everyone who
follows Jesus.

When life gets tough, come back to this passage
of scripture. God has great things planned for you!

• •

Father, help me remain hopeful!

Give God Your Trust

*God shall bring every work into judgment, with
every secret thing, whether it is good or evil.*
ECCLESIASTES 12:14 SKJV

• •

Solomon had seen—and lived—it all. At one time
the wisest man on earth, he had allowed his passion
for foreign women to lead him into idolatry. As the
wealthiest man alive, he had access to every imaginable
pleasure. He accomplished much good and yet failed
spectacularly.

Many believe, though, that Ecclesiastes was written
by an older Solomon, looking back on his life through
the lens of hard-won experience. This was a man who
could truly say, "Let us hear the conclusion of the whole
matter: Fear God and keep His commandments, for
this is the whole duty of man" (Ecclesiastes 12:13 SKJV).
With this priority, he could put the peaks and valleys
of life into proper perspective.

And so can we. No matter what you're going
through right now, remember that your highest mountain may soon become a valley and your darkest night
could give way to the noonday sun. Nothing about life
is certain—that honor belongs only to God. And He is
waiting for you to give Him your trust.

• •

*Lord God, help me to anchor my purpose in
You alone—everything else changes.*

When Faith Gets Stale

"Go and make followers of all the nations.
Baptize them in the name of the Father
and of the Son and of the Holy Spirit."
MATTHEW 28:19 NLV

• •

How do you live out your faith? You might go to church, say your prayers, and read your Bible—but is that all there is to Christianity?

So much of the New Testament describes believers sharing their faith in Christ. Even Jesus' last command was about going into the whole world to make disciples. Our faith begins with belief, but that belief is always bolstered by action.

At times, we get stuck in the same faith routines. If you ever feel like your prayers, Bible reading, or youth group experience are getting flat, consider Jesus' command to go spread the gospel.

Maybe you could start a Bible study at school or join a missions trip to share the good news of Jesus. Think about ways to *actively* live out your faith.

• •

Father, give me a passion to go, to live the
adventure of sharing the good news of Jesus.

God Uses Persecution

*I want you to know that what has happened to
me has helped spread the Good News. Everyone
around here knows why I am in prison. It is
because I preached about Jesus Christ.*
PHILIPPIANS 1:12–13 NLV

If you speak up for Jesus, or wear clothing with a Christian message, or are even known for attending a Bible-believing church, you may get guff from other kids. The apostle Paul felt a similar pressure—and he ended up in prison.

Writing from custody in Rome, Paul wanted his beloved Philippian brothers and sisters to see the bigger picture. He wanted them to understand why he had been arrested and detained—it was solely for preaching about the saving power of Jesus Christ.

Such troubles were not unusual for Paul. One time, while imprisoned in Philippi, Paul converted the jailer to faith in Christ. The man and his entire household were baptized, forming the nucleus of the Philippian church.

God often uses our persecution to advance His kingdom. We don't need to go looking for trouble—but when trials come, know that you don't need to worry. Stand firm in your faith, and God will use your troubles for good.

*Lord, I want to be like Paul—always
faithful, leading others to You.*

What Am I Doing Wrong?

*"You have planted much, but gather little.
You eat, but there is not enough to fill you.
You drink, but never have your fill. You put on
clothing, but no one is warm enough. You earn
money, but put it into a bag with holes."*

HAGGAI 1:6 NLV

• •

Hard times don't always indicate you're doing something wrong. Read Job's story for confirmation of that truth.

But sometimes difficulties *do* point to sin—or at least misplaced priorities—in our lives. Haggai's brief prophecy indicates that.

God's exiled people had returned to Jerusalem. They quickly improved their own homes but left God's temple in ruins. So the Lord not-so-gently defined their problem. "You look for much, but it turns out to be little," He said. "When you bring it home, I blow it away. Why? . . . Because My house lies waste, while each of you takes care of his own house" (Haggai 1:9 NLV).

When life is hard, it's not a bad idea to ask God, "What am I doing wrong?" If He shows you something specific, confess and change it. If there's nothing obvious, God may just be drawing you closer to Himself.

• •

Heavenly Father, please keep my whole focus on You.

Be Still and Know

"Be still and know that I am God. I will be exalted among the nations; I will be exalted in the earth."
PSALM 46:10 SKJV

. . . .

When life gets tough—when things are chaotic and you're stressed out—the best thing to do is be still. When you quiet your heart and mind, you can hear God's voice more clearly. He doesn't always speak in loud, booming tones. In fact, God rarely does that. Most of the time, you must listen carefully for His still, small voice.

You can be confident that God will take care of you. He proclaims that He will be honored in all the earth. One day every knee will bow and every tongue will declare that Jesus is Lord (Philippians 2:10–11). So any struggles you're experiencing right now are well within His power.

An old Sunday school song says, "My God is so big, so strong and so mighty, there's nothing my God cannot do!" When things are too big for *you* to handle, quiet yourself, listen for God's voice, and trust that He will take care of everything.

. . . .

Lord God, You are big and mighty. There's nothing you can't do. May I always listen for Your voice and trust You to act.

Justice Is Coming

*He who digs a pit shall fall into it, and whoever
breaks through a hedge, a serpent shall bite him.*
ECCLESIASTES 10:8 SKJV

• •

Ever seen the old *Road Runner* cartoons? The basic
premise is this: Wile E. Coyote tries to catch the title
character, fails, and gets humiliated in comical (and
usually painful) ways. Every time.

In a way, that's what happens to anyone who
schemes against God. Sure, we may not see the "back-
fire" immediately, but make no mistake—it's coming.

Depending on where you stand with God, this can
be either a comfort or a warning. If you're the victim
of another person's wickedness, you can rest assured
that justice will win the day. Your pain is temporary, and
the more you suffer, the greater your reward will be.
But if *you're* the one who's persecuting the innocent
and defying God's command, well. . .you'll soon find
yourself relating more to Mr. Coyote than you'd like.

And God's judgment is no laughing matter.

• •

*Lord, thank You for making sure righteousness prevails.
Help me to be patient while Your story unfolds—in the
end, I want to be on the right side of Your justice.*

Strong Finish

"But I am not worried about this. I do not think of my life as worth much, but I do want to finish the work the Lord Jesus gave me to do. My work is to preach the Good News of God's loving-favor."
Acts 20:24 NLV

● ●

You're a teenager—you're probably not thinking about the end of your life.

But nobody knows exactly how long their life is going to last. And even if you live a hundred years, you'll find they go very quickly. Even teen guys should be thinking of "the finish."

Every choice you make today contributes to the man you'll be at the end of your days. Careless, lazy, or disobedient choices will lead to trouble. Wise, Bible-based decision-making leads to blessing and life.

It's not weird or morbid to consider the end of your time on earth. In fact, it's a great exercise to stop and think who you really want to be as you head into eternity. A strong finish propels you into God's loving presence and is a great example for those left behind.

● ●

Lord God, help me to use my days on earth wisely, so if I live to be twenty or ninety, I can truly finish strong.

We Need Each Other

*Help each other. Speak day after day to each
other while it is still today so your heart will
not become hard by being fooled by sin.*
HEBREWS 3:13 NLV

You've probably heard someone say that "the Christian life isn't meant to be lived alone." God's Word does tell us, over and over again, that followers of Jesus need each other. Today's scripture says that will protect our hearts and keep us from falling into sin.

Satan can disguise himself as an angel of light (2 Corinthians 11:14). That means he's subtle as he tries to pull us away from God. The devil might try to make you think you should meet your own needs rather than depending on God. Satan may attempt to convince you that a sinful action is good or that you deserve some pleasure God has forbidden.

To make sure you don't fall for such lies, surround yourself with committed Christians. They will remind you of biblical truth while you do the same for them. We really do need each other.

Lord, I thank You for the believers You have placed in my life. Help us always to lead each other to Your truth.

Taking on Responsibility

"Do what the Lord your God tells you. Walk in His ways. Keep all His Laws and His Word, by what is written in the Law of Moses. Then you will do well in all that you do and in every place you go."

1 KINGS 2:3 NLV

As a teen guy, you're gaining freedom every day. Maybe not as fast as you'd like, but you're definitely moving toward adulthood. And while the opportunities are fun and exciting, some of the responsibilities are scary.

Should you go to college? If so, which one? Is it time to find a job? How can you balance school, work, church, and social life? What will happen when you're truly out on your own?

Today's scripture contains the words of King David, who was handing responsibilities over to his son Solomon. While David gave Solomon some very specific guidance later, this advice was universal, applicable even to us today. Job One is obeying God. Know what His Word says and do it.

You don't have to decide your entire future right now. Jobs, college, marriage—those things will happen in time. But knowing and obeying God is for right now. And that's something anyone can commit to.

Lord, help me to know and follow You.
Then I'll do well in whatever I do.

Make Time to Pray

Jesus came with them to a place called
Gethsemane. He said to them, "You sit
here while I go over there to pray."
MATTHEW 26:36 NLV

• •

Did you know that Jesus faced stresses like you do? That's an amazing aspect of our "God in the flesh": He experienced all the same struggles and pains that we do. He can relate fully to us because He knows what it's like to be mocked, abandoned, even physically abused.

How did Jesus deal with such pressures? Luke tells us that Jesus got away for private prayer: "He went away by Himself to pray in a desert" (Luke 5:16 NLV). This was a regular thing for Jesus, up to the night of the arrest and trial that led to His crucifixion.

As Christians, we are called to imitate Jesus. So make time to pray in a quiet, private place. When you struggle with grades or friendships or the future, pray. It's a great way to be like Jesus—and He will respond with help.

• •

Lord, there's a lot going on. I pray that You'll
help me make time to pray, then give me
the strength to do what I need to do.

Run for Your Life!

*And David said in his heart, "Now I shall perish
one day by the hand of Saul. There is nothing
better for me than that I should speedily
escape into the land of the Philistines."*
1 SAMUEL 27:1 SKJV

• •

Discover magazine once profiled a Kentucky woman
(known simply as SM) with a rare disorder that had
destroyed the part of her brain called the amygdala.
But SM doesn't mind. Through a strange twist of fate
and science, the disease has robbed her of only one
thing: the ability to feel fear.

Snakes? No problem. Halloween haunted house?
Won't bat an eyelash. Scary movies? Scary for some,
maybe, but not for her.

Unfortunately, most of us aren't like this woman.
Even some of the Bible's greatest heroes—David, Elijah,
Jesus—experienced anxiety when in danger. It's a nat-
ural human response.

Though there's no way to escape fear, God has
provided a way to overcome it—by trusting in His
promises. He has assured His children of an eternity
with Him, and nothing will thwart that plan.

Isn't that a reason to be fearless?

• •

*Lord God, may my anxiety never cloud my
acknowledgment of Your goodness. You're
bigger than anything that scares me.*

Find a Mentor

Joash did what was right in the eyes of the Lord all his days, because Jehoiada the religious leader taught him.
2 KINGS 12:2 NLV

• •

Joash had a rough beginning, to say the least. Though he was the son of a king, things went south when his father died. Joash's grandmother, who wanted to rule Judah, started killing any family members who could claim the throne. An aunt hid baby Joash for the next six years, when the high priest Jehoiada pronounced him king. Yes, Joash was *seven* years old.

Under Jehoiada's leadership, Joash started strong. Though he wasn't perfect, he did much good. Sadly, though, after Jehoiada died, Joash listened to sinful government officials who encouraged him to worship false gods (2 Chronicles 24:17–19).

Our world is full of people who will happily pull you away from God. That's why it's so important to have support. Seek out Christian friends your own age— but also look for an older man as a mentor. A mature Christian man will be happy to serve as your Jehoiada.

• •

Lord, I know I need good, strong Christian men in my life. Please lead me to the ones who will help me stay true to You.

Look Up!

Therefore, I will look to the L<small>ORD</small>. I will wait for the God of my salvation. My God will hear me.
M<small>ICAH</small> 7:7 <small>SKJV</small>

• •

Few people had harder lives than God's prophets. They carried tough messages to tough people and often experienced tough results. Take Micah, for instance.

Though he made the beautiful prediction of Jesus' birth in Bethlehem (Micah 5:2), he was soon saying, "Woe is me! . . . The good man has perished from the earth, and there is no one upright among men. They all lie in wait for blood. Every man hunts his brother with a net. . . . The son dishonors the father, the daughter rises up against her mother, the daughter-in-law against her mother-in-law. A man's enemies are the men of his own house" (Micah 7:1–2, 6 <small>SKJV</small>).

In such a world, Micah could only look up, as he indicated in today's scripture. What would that accomplish? "When I fall, I shall arise," he said. "When I sit in darkness, the L<small>ORD</small> shall be a light for me" (Micah 7:8 <small>SKJV</small>).

• •

Heavenly Father, when this world is crazy, remind me to look to You. You always make sense!

Love Your Brothers

As you live God-like, be kind to Christian
brothers and love them.
2 Peter 1:7 nlv

Toward the end of his life, the apostle Peter shared some parting thoughts to a group of churches in Asia Minor, the area of modern-day Turkey. Knowing his death was approaching, Peter wanted to make a final challenge to his fellow believers. That challenge was *love*.

Many guys struggle to express love. But even if it's hard to *say* it, make the effort to *show* it. Keep an eye out for friends in need of help, then step in with a text of encouragement, a gift of money, or your physical presence to lend a hand. Have you ever had someone step up when you were in need? That's what Peter wants us to do to "live God-like."

Love makes a huge impact on a person who's struggling. But don't forget that Jesus said, "We are more happy when we give than when we receive" (Acts 20:35 nlv). Talk about a win-win.

Father, help me to love my friends and treat
them with kindness. I want to be a great example
of Your love to the people around me.

Stay Awake

Keep awake! Do not sleep like others. Watch and keep your minds awake to what is happening.
1 Thessalonians 5:6 nlv

• •

Have you heard of "The Secret Life of Walter Mitty"? It's a famous short story about a man who lives a mundane life but escapes into exciting daydreams—he's a navy pilot in wartime, a world-class surgeon, a man calmly facing a firing squad.

At some time or another, we all get to daydreaming. We think about doing something else, living somewhere else, being someone else. Of course, teenagers need to spend time considering their future—but we don't dare get stuck in our dreaming. The apostle Paul calls us to attention, blowing a bugle to keep us alert. Christians need to know what's going on around them and how God is calling them to live.

If anybody should be in touch with reality, it's Christians—we know the God who created reality. So stay awake. Don't dream your life away. Live in the here-and-now, and accomplish good things for God.

• •

Lord God, wake me up to the life You've called me to live. I want it to count!

Why?

Uzza put out his hand to hold the ark, for the oxen stumbled. And the anger of the LORD was kindled against Uzza, and. . .he died there before God. And David was displeased.
1 CHRONICLES 13:9–11 SKJV

● ●

Shocked, David stared at Uzza's body on the ground. *Why would God do such a thing?* he wondered. *Uzza meant no harm!*

Interestingly, these questions are never truly resolved. Uzza disobeyed, so he died. The story goes no further. Was this incident a stark reminder for future generations not to tamper with God's holiness? Did Uzza have some secret sin in his life that compounded God's judgment? We'll never know.

David was confused. But despite his inability to understand God's ways, he still followed God. So should we.

Every day, we see troubling things happening. It's easy to ask why God allows them. But as David—and many biblical individuals—learned, God's ways are "unsearchable" and "past finding out" (Romans 11:33 SKJV).

God has His own reasons for everything He does. Our job is simply to trust Him.

● ●

Thank You for knowing what's best, Father, even when I don't understand. Help me trust You no matter what.

Helping Others

*God. . .will not forget the work you did to help the
Christians and the work you are still doing to help
them. This shows your love for Christ. We want
each one of you to keep on working to the end.*
HEBREWS 6:10–11 NLV

Have you ever struggled with a sin and started to lose
hope? Sometimes when we give in to temptation, we
begin to wonder if we're truly saved.

But ask yourself this question: Do you love other
Christians? Are you doing anything to help and encour-
age fellow believers? Do you serve in church or a
Christian ministry? These are all good signs.

When you truly love the church—which is simply
all the followers of Christ—it indicates your love for
Jesus Himself. Of course you should take your own
sin seriously and fight against it. But don't let Satan
make you question your faith after you have confessed
and repented. The apostle Paul would say, "Keep on
working and helping fellow Christians along the path-
way to heaven."

*Lord, as I fight against my own sin nature,
I want to work for the members of Your
kingdom. Use me in any way You see fit.*

When You Don't Know What to Say

In the same way, the Holy Spirit helps us where we are weak. We do not know how to pray or what we should pray for, but the Holy Spirit prays to God for us with sounds that cannot be put into words. God knows the hearts of men. He knows what the Holy Spirit is thinking. The Holy Spirit prays for those who belong to Christ the way God wants Him to pray.
ROMANS 8:26–27 NLV

• •

There will be times when you're so angry, sad, or confused that words simply won't form in your mind or mouth. It can even happen when you want to pray.

Don't worry if this happens to you. It's a common human condition. Why else would the apostle Paul write about it?

The good news is that even in your worst moments, the Holy Spirit is praying for you, in you, and with you. Keep trying, even when the words won't come out. God knows your heart, and He's already helping.

• •

Heavenly Father, You know my heart and my thoughts. When I can't put words together, I know Your Spirit is communicating for me. Thank You!

Unexpected Friends

*The people on the island were very kind
to us. It was raining and cold. They made
a fire so we could get warm.*
ACTS 28:2 NLV

On his way to Rome for a trial before Caesar, the apostle Paul was shipwrecked—along with 275 other people. But thanks to God's miraculous intervention, not a single person was lost.

Though it may be less dramatic, the response of the people of Malta was just as much a "God thing." When bedraggled people started washing up on shore, the residents of the island came out to help. They showed kindness to the castaways, building a fire for their comfort.

God has His own people all around the world, and they create a family that is ready and willing to serve a brother in need. And God can even use unbelievers to His purposes and the benefit of His own family.

When you're in a tough spot, ask God for help. Then watch to see what unexpected friends show up.

*Lord God, when I need support, I know You'll
send exactly the right person. And in better
times, please use me to be that person!*

Your Power Source

*But we have this treasure in earthen
vessels, that the excellency of the power
may be from God and not from us.*
2 Corinthians 4:7 skjv

• •

Do you ever feel inadequate as a Christian? Maybe
the stresses of school, family life, and increasing
responsibility have eroded your self-confidence. Maybe
you struggle with temptations, doubts, depression, or
other spiritual and emotional assailants. *I'm just not cut
out for this*, you might think.

That's true, actually. Nobody's "cut out" for life's
trials. In God's eyes, our weakness is kind of the point.
If we were strong enough to handle everything, how
could God ever be glorified? That's why God whittled
Gideon's army down from thirty-two thousand to just
three hundred men (Judges 7:1–7), and that's why
Paul wrote that God's "strength is made perfect in
weakness" (2 Corinthians 12:9 skjv).

God knew that you'd never be able to handle life
alone—it's why He wants you to lean on Him.

• •

*Lord, I'm grateful that You don't rely on my strength
to accomplish Your plans. Please work through
me, and remind me to always give You the glory.*

All Things New

"Those of you who are hungry now are happy,
because you will be filled. Those of you who have
sorrow now are happy, because you will laugh."
Luke 6:21 nlv

If you've ever faced real hunger, you know how distressing it is. And if you've faced real sorrow, you know the fear that you'll never be happy again.

But Jesus wants you to know something: a day is coming when you will never be hungry, either literally or spiritually. And you will never be sad again.

In the new heavens and new earth, " 'God's home is with men. He will live with them. They will be His people. God Himself will be with them. He will be their God. God will take away all their tears. There will be no more death or sorrow or crying or pain. All the old things have passed away' " (Revelation 21:3–4 nlv). All things will be made new.

Any suffering we experience in this life is temporary. Someday, possibly very soon, you will be filled. You will laugh. . .never to suffer again!

Lord, in this broken world, give me an
eternal perspective. I can't wait until You
come back and make all things new.

Do I Have to, Lord?

"Lie on your left side and lay the iniquity of the house of Israel on it; you shall bear their iniquity according to the number of the days that you shall lie on it. For I have laid on you the years of their iniquity; according to the number of the days."
EZEKIEL 4:4–5 SKJV

• •

Ever get restless under God's commands? Even as Christians, we struggle with temptation. We often want to do our own thing and avoid what He says.

Imagine being Ezekiel. God told him to act out the upcoming siege of Jerusalem. The prophet was to build a little model of the city, then lay down beside it for 430 days—390 on his left side and 40 on his right—to indicate the years of Israel and Judah's sin. Ezekiel would be on public display for well over a year. *Really, God?*

Our Christian life is a paradox—God frees us from sin to make us His slaves. Just remember: any sinful pleasures we choose to pursue may very well destroy us. But anything we give up for God will be richly rewarded in this life or the next. . .or both.

• •

*Lord, Your ways are right. Empower me
to follow You wholeheartedly.*

True Happiness

*Happy is the man who does not walk in the way
sinful men tell him to, or stand in the path of
sinners, or sit with those who laugh at the truth.*

PSALM 1:1 NLV

• •

Sometimes life is harder because of the people we hang out with. Of course, you can't avoid every unbeliever, nor should you. As the apostle Paul said, "To get away from people like that you would have to leave this world!" (1 Corinthians 5:10 NLV).

But if you've ever gone to church camp or a youth conference, you know that spending time with other people who love Jesus fuels your faith in a way few other things can.

True happiness comes from walking in the light. When we walk with other committed Christians, we find challenge and encouragement that make us better people. We should still interact with unbelievers in hopes of pointing them to Jesus. But we should spend more quality time with Christians.

Choose wisely who you hang out with—your decision can lead to hardship or happiness.

• •

*Lord God, help me to share Your love with
people who don't know You. But guide me into
quality time with like-minded believers.*

Impossible Mercy

For he who has shown no mercy shall have judgment without mercy; and mercy rejoices over judgment.
JAMES 2:13 SKJV

• •

The year was 1943. US Army Air Forces bombardier Louis Zamperini had just been taken captive by Japanese sailors. . .and they were not friendly.

For nearly two years, Zamperini endured terrible beatings. For four years after his release, nightmares and dark thoughts of revenge swirled in his mind.

But in 1949, Zamperini attended a Billy Graham crusade. As he listened, something in his heart began to change. Zamperini cried out to God for salvation—and God gave him a portion of His own mercy. The hatred and anger and nightmares disappeared, replaced by an overwhelming urge to forgive his captors.

One by one, Zamperini visited the Japanese guards who had made his life miserable for so long. As he told his stunned audience of his newfound love, many of the captors gave their lives to Christ as well.

His story is extreme, but it shows what God wants us all to do. This is "mercy rejoicing over judgment."

• •

Lord, You forgave those who nailed You to the cross—the least I can do is forgive people who treat me harshly. Grant me strength to obey.

A Chain of Beauty

Hear your father's teaching, my son, and do not turn away from your mother's teaching. For they are a glory to your head and a chain of beauty around your neck. My son, if sinners try to lead you into sin, do not go with them.
PROVERBS 1:8–10 NLV

If your parents are Christians, you know the benefits. They've helped you understand the Bible and taught you to pray, modeling faithful behavior to you. If you don't live in a Christian home, you know the challenges. But you're never alone—Jesus has promised to be with you.

No matter what your background, today's scripture offers wisdom. If your parents are good, committed Christians, they want to see you grow into the image of Christ. Obey them, even when you don't understand, and you'll save yourself a lot of heartache. If your parents aren't Christians, you should still obey them, unless they tell you to do something sinful. But you can look for a godly mentor to help you grow, and begin praying about your household down the road.

Lord, I thank You for older believers who can help me in my pursuit of Christ. Please shape me into the kind of man who will lead his own household well.

You Can Come Back

Peter remembered the words Jesus had said
to him, "Before a rooster crows, you will
say three times you do not know Me." Peter
went outside and cried with loud cries.
MATTHEW 26:75 NLV

Have you ever really blown it? Maybe you carelessly shared someone's secret or you followed the crowd into something foolish. A guilty conscience can be devastating. It might feel like you can never come back from your failure.

Peter knew that feeling. Though Jesus had renamed him "Rock" (the meaning of Peter), this leader of the disciples found himself in a deep emotional pit after Jesus' arrest. Peter had earlier declared—publicly and loudly—that He would never deny His Lord. In fact Peter said, he would *die* with Christ. But then he fearfully insisted three times that he didn't even know Jesus.

Peter was inconsolable. But after the resurrection, Jesus restored Peter to leadership. He would soon preach a sermon that led three thousand people to accept Christ, a key moment in the growth of the church.

God is all about second chances. He is ready to forgive no matter how many times or how badly you've sinned. You can come back.

Father, thank You for forgiving all my sin through Jesus.

Watch What You Do

Do not give any part of your body for sinful use.
Instead, give yourself to God as a living person
who has been raised from the dead. Give every
part of your body to God to do what is right.
ROMANS 6:13 NLV

• •

It's a common temptation: to use our bodies in sinful ways as a means of coping with our struggles. That's been true throughout human history, but it's especially difficult today with the explosion of pornography, drugs, gambling, and other addictive behaviors. Society lowers our standards and desensitizes us to what's appropriate and what's not.

As young Christian men, we have to do better! It's so easy to let our minds (and bodies) wander, especially when life is tough. But God calls us to be "living sacrifices" to Him (Romans 12:1)—to control our bodies and use them for good things. Those good things may be tough—but they're far better than the easy, destructive path that so many people are traveling.

God calls you to excellence. Watch what you do!

• •

Father, I give You my body, mind, and spirit.
Help me never to use my body for sinful
things. Empower me to do good.

Humble in Troubled Times

"Do you seek great things for yourself? Do not seek them, for behold, I will bring evil on all flesh," says the LORD. "But I will give your life to you as plunder in all places where you go."
JEREMIAH 45:5 SKJV

Jeremiah 45 is a very short chapter in a very long book. Four of its five verses are specifically directed to Baruch, who was Jeremiah's scribe—the man who wrote down the prophet's messages from God. The Lord wanted Baruch to know that judgment was coming on his sinful nation, so he shouldn't expect great things for himself. That was certainly bad news. But God offered good news too—Baruch's life would be spared from the devastation of the coming Babylonian invasion.

What does this twenty-five-hundred-year-old story mean to us? Well, we live in tough times as well. Our hopes and dreams and aspirations may be derailed by circumstances beyond our control. But those circumstances are always under *God's* control, and we can always trust Him to do right.

However the times may be, stay humble. Pursue the dreams God gives you, but hold them loosely. He may override them for His own purposes.

Lord God, You know best. Help me to be faithful in good times and bad.

Is It True?

These Jews were more willing to understand than those in the city of Thessalonica. They were very glad to hear the Word of God, and they looked into the Holy Writings to see if those things were true.
ACTS 17:11 NLV

• •

This world can be a tricky place to sort out what is right or wrong. When close friends throw their support behind a philosophy or a cause, we might want to follow along. Many ideas sound good at first. But it's always wise to ask yourself if the idea is true. And the only way to know that is by measuring everything against God's Word, the Bible.

When the apostle Paul traveled to the Berea, a city in what is now Greece, the people were excited to hear his message. But they didn't accept Paul's teaching until they had compared it against scripture.

"There is a way which looks right to a man," the Proverbs say, "but its end is the way of death" (14:12). That's an important warning for every follower of Jesus. When you're presented with a new idea, make sure it aligns with the truth and reality of God's Word.

• •

Lord, please make Your thoughts my thoughts, and Your ways my ways.

Shamed for Jesus

"You are happy when men hate you and do not want you around and put shame on you because you trust in Me. Be glad in that day. Be full of joy for your reward is much in heaven."
Luke 6:22–23 NLV

If you are a public Christian, scripture says you will be hated, mocked, and shamed for trusting in Christ. Never forget that the world hated Jesus Himself.

Being shamed and hated is evidence of who you are in Christ. But it's a small price to pay for what you have coming one day in eternity. In today's scripture, Jesus says your reward will be "much."

Who knows exactly what that reward will be like? But you can be sure it'll be far better than anything you could receive here on earth. For now, you have two choices: you can be uptight about what people say about you, or you can be glad when they hate you for Jesus' sake—because a heavenly reward awaits you.

Lord Jesus, I can't thank You enough for what You did for me on the cross. I'll remember that joy anytime someone criticizes me for trusting in You.

When the Burden Is Too Heavy

"This is the word of the LORD to Zerubbabel,
saying, 'Not by might, nor by power, but
by My Spirit,' says the LORD of hosts."
ZECHARIAH 4:6 SKJV

• •

At times, most everyone gets overwhelmed. The task is too big, the burden too heavy.

Zerubbabel was leader of the exiled Jews who returned to Jerusalem some five hundred years before Jesus was born. He laid the foundation for a temple to replace the one destroyed by the Babylonian army decades earlier. Apparently, Zerubbabel felt a bit stressed by the job, because God told the prophet Zechariah to pass along the message of today's scripture.

Though that was a specific promise to a specific man at a specific time, there's a principle in it for all of us: it is only by God's power that we accomplish anything. Jesus reminded us that we are simply branches connected to Him as the life-giving vine (John 15:5). And when we "abide" in Him, we can cast every anxiety on His very broad shoulders (1 Peter 5:7).

• •

Lord Jesus, I give You my heavy struggles.
I know You can handle them easily.

Made Right!

For all men have sinned and have missed the shining-greatness of God. Anyone can be made right with God by the free gift of His loving-favor. It is Jesus Christ Who bought them with His blood and made them free from their sins.
ROMANS 3:23–24 NLV

• •

You might want to *think* you're good, but deep down, you know the truth. You've sinned. Everyone has.

Sin affects us all, and it brings with it regret, guilt, stress, pain. . .all kinds of trouble. Isn't it nice to know that Jesus can make that sin go away? His work on the cross means anyone can be right with God the Father through simple faith.

What's weighing on you right now? Shame? Anxiety? Fear? Not only does the blood of Jesus make you free from sin, it can break the power of sin's effects too.

So when life is beating you up, know that God has made a way out. When you feel like you're trapped in sin, know that you have an escape route. Don't ever think of yourself as hopeless when Jesus offers the way out.

• •

Lord, I thank You for Your forgiveness! May I take full advantage of Your way out of my sin and shame.

Already, but Not Yet

Jesus answered, "My kingdom is not of this world."
JOHN 18:36 SKJV

. . . .

Sometimes preachers talk about the "already, but not yet." The puzzling phrase is just a way of expressing the profound truth of today's verse.

We don't live in a perfect world—as any quick scan of the headlines will tell you. Maybe you've even experienced some tragedy yourself. The idea of God's kingdom being here on earth can be downright confusing. That seems so at odds with our observation that it can't possibly be true, right?

Wrong. As Jesus explained, God's kingdom isn't something you can see or touch yet. It's a spiritual kingdom, and His throne lies within each of our hearts. That's the "already" part.

The "not yet," naturally, lies in the future. One day, our dreams of perfection will be realized, and every pain we've suffered will be washed away in an eternity of joy with our Maker. This future isn't a "maybe." It's guaranteed for all who will join in.

Are you "already" part of God's kingdom?

. . . .

Thank You, God, for assuring me of heaven.
I can't wait until the "not yet" arrives!

Happiness Is a Gift

*Where there is no understanding of the Word
of the Lord, the people do whatever they want
to, but happy is he who keeps the law.*
PROVERBS 29:18 NLV

• •

You don't have to look hard at culture to realize that people, in general, do not have an understanding of God's Word. Many believe the Bible is outdated, no longer applicable since humanity is "more enlightened now." Some believe scripture is actually a source of trouble. Meanwhile, sin is celebrated.

If you try to live according to biblical principles, the world will do all it can to make you miserable. People will mock and shun you. But though the world hates your beliefs, holding firm to biblical teaching actually brings happiness.

Did you see that in today's scripture? Your happiness isn't dependent on what anyone else thinks or does. It's a gift from God, who blesses everyone who follows Him faithfully.

• •

*Lord, when the world attacks me for
following You, remind me that faithfulness
to Your Word brings happiness.*

Tired of Doing Good?

Do not let yourselves get tired of doing good. If we do not give up, we will get what is coming to us at the right time.

GALATIANS 6:9 NLV

. . . .

Have you ever felt like obeying God and doing good gets you nowhere? You study hard and get a C on the test, while other kids get an A by cheating. You stand up for God and people call you names. You find a wallet full of cash but know you have to give it back to its owner.

The Christian life can be frustrating. Faith is a battlefield, and you can get tired carrying a sword all the time.

In today's scripture, the apostle Paul urged the Christians of Galatia to hang in there. He saw they were getting weary but told them to keep doing good anyway. God would reward them at the proper time. . . and His timing is perfect.

This is true for us too. This world and true Christianity are incompatible, and you will feel pressure for being different. But your difference is a shining light in a dark world. Keep shining. God promises it will ultimately be worth it.

. . . .

Father, sometimes I just want to fit in. Please help me to stay the course, though, following You with my whole heart.

Honor God, He Honors You

*In this way, the name of the Lord Jesus Christ
will be honored by you and you will be honored
by Him. It is through the loving-favor of
our God and of the Lord Jesus Christ.*
2 Thessalonians 1:12 nlv

When you commit to doing God's will, no matter what, He will honor you. In this world, it's easy to trip and fall. But if your goal is to honor God, He will pick you up and help you get back on track.

In the passage that includes today's scripture, the apostle Paul encouraged the believers in Thessalonica to keep doing the good things they were doing. The Christian's mission hasn't changed from then to now. We are to know Christ and to make disciples for Him. In other words, we are to reflect Jesus to our world.

When you serve the Lord, life will get tough. But God will never leave you alone (Hebrews 13:5). So go ahead—spread the love of Jesus to your family, friends, neighbors, and coworkers. The struggle is worth it. . . and with God in your corner, nothing can stop you.

*God, help me to serve You consistently. I want to
honor You and receive Your honor in return.*

Finish Well

Look to yourselves, that we don't lose those things that we have worked for, but that we receive a full reward.
2 JOHN 8 SKJV

• •

Imagine this scenario: You've studied for weeks for a final exam. A scholarship depends entirely on how you score tomorrow. But, confident that you've mastered the material, you go to bed and sleep peacefully.

When your alarm goes off, you sit up in bed thinking, *This is it.* But as you glance out the window, you notice it's raining. *Perfect sleeping weather*, you tell yourself. You switch off your alarm and lie back down. Who needs exams, anyway?

Crazy as that sounds, it represents what a lot of Christians do. Many of us spend large chunks of our lives attending church, reading the Bible, listening to good music and teaching, only to disregard what we've learned when the crunch comes.

Life will get tough. You will sometimes be tempted to throw in the towel. Don't! When you've come so far already, be sure to finish well.

• •

Lord, I know You're teaching me to follow You.
May I put this learning to good use every day—
I don't want to miss out on my reward.

Hiding from Real Life

*The people of Athens and those visiting
from far countries used all their time in
talking or hearing some new thing.*
ACTS 17:21 NLV

• •

Have you heard the expression "bury your head in the sand"? It means you ignore the real issue and pretend everything is okay. It's a common human response to stress.

In our world, people bury their heads in the sand by endlessly scrolling through social media, playing video games, and binge-watching television series. Meanwhile, the challenges of real life continue, no matter how much we may wish them away.

When the apostle Paul traveled to Athens, he ran into a group of people "who used all their time in talking or hearing some new thing." They weren't engaging with real life, and Paul tried to get them to consider the reality of sin and salvation through Jesus Christ.

If you find yourself trying to hide from real life, it's time to pray. Ask God to give you the strength to get your head out of the sand. Then get to work.

• •

*Father, when I want to avoid my problems, please
help me to face them—in Your strength.*

No Need to Fear

The man who reads this Book and listens to it
being read and obeys what it says will be happy.
REVELATION 1:3 NLV

The first time you read the Bible's last book, it might scare you. Revelation describes what will happen to all those people who don't heed scripture's warnings. They face terrible judgments, including eternal separation from God. But Revelation also promises blessings to those who repent and follow Jesus. Obeying God leads to true happiness.

John, who received end-times visions from Jesus, wrote of heaven, "I saw many people. No one could tell how many there were. They were from every nation and from every family and from every kind of people and from every language. They were standing before the throne and before the Lamb" (Revelation 7:9 NLV). If you have accepted Jesus as Savior, you're a part of that crowd. This picture is of *your* future as a Christian. With possibly billions of other believers, you'll be shouting, "We are saved from the punishment of sin by our God Who sits on the throne and by the Lamb!" (Revelation 7:10 NLV).

There is no need to fear the future.

Lord, I don't fear the end because You've given me
a glimpse of what's coming. And it's incredible!

You Are Chosen and Loved

Even before the world was made, God chose us for Himself because of His love. He planned that we should be holy and without blame as He sees us.
EPHESIANS 1:4 NLV

• •

Did you know that God knew you before you were born? You were on His heart before He even created life. He knew the plans He had for you before He laid the foundations of the earth. He knew the good, the bad, and the ugly before you had a chance to decide on one or the other. Yet He still gave you breath.

When life beats you down, it's easy to give up. When the odds are stacked against you, it's easy to question your very existence. But no matter what's going on in your head, remember this: God chose you! And He chose you "for Himself because of His love."

Now *you* get to choose—to see yourself the way God sees you. If you do, you'll find that the troubles of this life lose much of their power.

• •

Father, You know everything about me yet You love me. Help me to see myself as You see me—chosen from before time began.

Scripture Index

Another Great Devotional for Teen Guys!

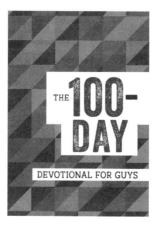

The 100-Day Devotional for Guys offers relatable, real-life wisdom and inspiration for everyday living. You'll encounter page after page of biblical truths you can apply to every area of your life—with topics like Popularity, Doubt, the Media, Stress, Self-Image, Priorities, Contentment, and much more.

Paperback / 978-1-63609-367-3